Praise for *Oh Boy, You're Having a Girl*

"As the father of a daughter, I wish I'd read this very funny book sooner, if only to know that it's okay for a grown man to wear a tutu."

—Dave Barry

"Somehow, Brian Klems has taken one of the most traumatic situations known to a father—having a daughter—and made it into something so completely hilarious you'll laugh until you've got oxygen deprivation!"

—W. Bruce Cameron, author of *8 Simple Rules for Dating My Teenage Daughter*

"Required reading for any parent who doesn't know pants from leggings."

—Dan Zevin, author of *Dan Gets a Minivan: Life at the Intersection of Dude and Dad*

"This hilarious book is a must-read for all dads who have a daughter—I should know, I'm one of them. It's smart, relatable, and will keep you from panicking when everything around you turns pink."

—Chuck Sambuchino, bestselling humorist (*How to Survive a Garden Gnome Attack*) and father of a daughter

"I loved *Oh Boy, You're Having a Girl*. As a proud father of three girls, I found myself smiling (and laughing) throu~~gh~~ ~~it~~. Klems delivers more often than a group of si~~ster~~ ~~wives~~

—John Pfeiffer, author of th~~~~ *Dad!*

OH BOY,
YOU'RE HAVING A
Girl

OH BOY, YOU'RE HAVING A *Girl*

A DAD'S SURVIVAL GUIDE TO RAISING DAUGHTERS

BRIAN A. KLEMS

TheLifeOfDad.com

adamsmedia
Avon, Massachusetts

Published by
Adams Media, a division of F+W Media, Inc.
57 Littlefield Street, Avon, MA 02322. U.S.A.
www.adamsmedia.com

ISBN 10: 1-4405-4545-6
ISBN 13: 978-1-4405-4545-0
eISBN 10: 1-4405-4546-4
eISBN 13: 978-1-4405-4546-7

Printed in the United States of America.

10 9 8 7 6 5 4 3 2 1

This publication is designed to provide accurate and authoritative information
with regard to the subject matter covered. It is sold with the understanding that
the publisher is not engaged in rendering legal, accounting, or other professional
advice. If legal advice or other expert assistance is required, the services of a
competent professional person should be sought.
—From a *Declaration of Principles* jointly adopted by a Committee of the
American Bar Association and a Committee of Publishers and Associations

Many of the designations used by manufacturers and sellers to distinguish their
product are claimed as trademarks. Where those designations appear in this book
and F+W Media was aware of a trademark claim, the designations have been
printed with initial capital letters.

This book is available at quantity discounts for bulk purchases.
For information, please call 1-800-289-0963.

To Ella, Anna, and Mia. I wouldn't trade you for anything in the world, not even partial ownership of the Cincinnati Reds.

Contents

INTRODUCTION

If you're a guy and you've opened this book, you either *have a daughter*, are on the verge of *having a daughter*, or are in the delivery room hoping that the sweet bundle of joy that just emerged from your wife somehow, someway, spontaneously grows a penis. I am here to tell you: That almost never happens.

One thing is certainly clear—you're out of your element. You've spent all your life being a guy, developing skills like chest-bumping and growing a mustache, all of which provide zero education on how to raise a girl. In fact, your friends, who are acutely aware of how little you know about girls, are probably still unclear as to how you landed such a smart, beautiful wife. They definitely won't believe you when you tell them that you "wowed her" by finishing third in your legacy fantasy baseball league. (They also will remind you that your team, "The Man-Eating Sweater Vests," actually finished fifth.)

I know, things don't look pretty at this point. You're starting down a path littered with tip-toeing ballet shoes and make-believe tea (though, when it's poured from a pot brewed by sweet little daughter hands, you'll be surprised at how quickly you'll learn to love it). You are going to schedule emergency eye doctor appointments to confirm (or deny) that you are suffering from a rare condition that allows you to see only shades of pink. And, you'll spend every second of every hour of every day trying to convince your wife that the outside of your house is in dire need of a seventeen-foot-wide moat filled with alligators and fire-breathing dragons. (NOTE: I've read that doing this increases your property value and saves you on homeowners' insurance.)

But before you start to panic and say something crazy to your wife like, "Are you sure this baby is mine?" or "I liked the way LeBron handled his exit from Cleveland," hear me out. Raising a daughter is one of the biggest challenges you will ever experience as a guy—but it's also one of the most rewarding.

All joking aside, daughters really are the best. I have three of them and I wouldn't have it any other way. They are responsible for most of my laughs and smiles. They are the reason I get excited when a new *Dora the Explorer* special is on TV. They are the reason I work so hard each and every day to make the world a better place.

Still, raising girls isn't a challenge you can take lightly. Trust me, I know.

At the very young male age of twenty-seven, I started picturing what it'd be like to have a family because my wife told me it was time to start picturing what it'd be like to have a family. So I did. I imagined a yard, with freshly cut grass and manicured hedges thanks to my eldest son, who could give his old man a run for his money in an arm-wrestling competition. I imagined sharing a few laughs with my middle son as we drove around the fairway, pretending that our tee shots actually landed somewhere other than "out of bounds." And I imagined coaching my youngest son on his way to a Little League championship, remaining calm and composed, even though he's clearly unaware that his batting helmet is on backward.

For the first time, I could see myself as a father. And a moderately okay one at that. It made me a little less scared of parenthood.

Of course, everything unraveled a year later when my first daughter was born. And then my *second* daughter was born. And then my *third* daughter was . . . see a pattern here? Within the blink of an eye, I went from dreams of arm wrestling and Little

League to being the proud father of three daughters under the age of five. I had no one to blame but my wife, who I'm pretty sure willed herself to have girls just to punish me for leaving globs of toothpaste in the bathroom sink.

Despite a brief period of initial panic, I've lived through it. (In fact, I've learned to love it!) And I want to help *you* survive it (and love it) too. I've learned a lot during my first five years of having daughters. I hope through my experiences, advice, and wisdom, you'll learn to rise to the challenge when your daughter requires help naming all the Disney princesses, or asks you, in front of your softball buddies, "Dad, where are your boobs?" (Trust me, this will happen, but we'll get to that later.) As it turns out, I didn't need arm wrestling and Little League to be a great dad or a happy family man. I've actually come to love—okay, tolerate—ballet, pink, and Dora. Now I wouldn't change my life for anything.

By the end of this book, you won't feel nearly as terrified as you did when the doctor uttered those five life-changing words, "OH BOY, IT'S A GIRL!" In fact, you will start to feel *lucky* that you have daughters—after all, they are called "Daddy's Girls" for a reason.

But I'd still consider building that moat.

Chapter 1

It's a Girl!

(AND YOU CAN'T NAME HER MEGATRON)

People always say how difficult labor is. They tell you horror stories about uncomfortable delivery rooms, hours of pain, and a menu consisting of nothing but ice chips. I want to put you at ease a little by letting you know that these people—and I want to be perfectly clear on this—are complete and total liars. I found labor to be quite easy and painless, aside from a mild papercut I sustained while filling out insurance forms.

When our labor story began, I was visiting my parents, showing off my new MacBook Pro laptop—a computer that is so cool, it took the head cheerleader to prom and got to second base—twice! (NOTE: Don't let your daughter date a MacBook Pro.) I called my wife to brag and to see what time she'd be leaving the office, and our conversation went something like this:

Wife: "I think I might be going into labor."

Me: "Are you serious!?!"

Wife: "I'm going to send out a few more e-mails and finish up some odds and ends first . . ."

Me: "Are you crazy!?! Come home now!"

Wife: "Oh, I just received an e-mail forward from Jennifer. Subject line says 'Funniest video ever.' I better watch that real quick."

Me: "Are you insane!?! COME HOME NOW!"

Wife: <laughter>

Me: "Okay, send it to me."

The next twenty minutes were the longest of my life. I paced around the house. Was she coming home? Was she tidying her desk? Was she glued to her work computer studying the fine art of how to give her husband an amazing footrub.[1] My mind ran wild because, sometime soon, I was going to be a father for the very first time. I couldn't wait to meet my son—at this point, I had never considered that I'd be having anything other than a son. Well, one time I did imagine what it'd be like if my wife delivered a monkey

---

[1] This is a completely acceptable reason for wives to stay late at work, whether in labor or not.

(best daydream ever). And, because my wife wouldn't allow me to find out the gender of the baby ahead of time, I was still assuming it was a boy.

Finally, her car pulled into our driveway. When my lovely wife walked through the door, she asked me to call the doctor. I did.

"*Yeah, doc, the contractions are about thirty minutes apart. . . . Yeah, they do look pretty painful. . . . No, I don't think that the Cincinnati Reds have enough pieces in their bullpen to make a serious run at the playoffs this year, but you never know . . . You like that guy!? He's a bum! I'd trade him! . . . okay.*" (I hang up the phone.)

My wife, bent over in severe pain, turns to me. "What'd he say?"

If you're ever around a pregnant woman on the verge of having a baby, here is some important advice. The last thing she wants to hear is, *I know you're in pain. Turns out the pain is going to get worse . . . and happen more frequently . . . and when it gets as bad as you think it'll get, it'll actually get much worse. When it gets THAT bad and contractions are only about a* SportsCenter *commercial break–length apart, then we can call the doctor again and ASK for permission to go to the hospital.*

Unless you desire a black eye in the post-birth family photos, it's best to give her the abbreviated version of your conversation with the doc and then quickly change the subject: "I don't know. I think he was drunk. Who's in the mood for Taco Bell?"

IT'S SHOWTIME

When we finally got the okay to go to the hospital, we roamed the halls of the labor and delivery floor. I saw banner after banner on door after door. "It's a boy!" "It's a boy!" they all said. Like all expecting fathers whose wives wouldn't let us find out what we were having at an earlier ultrasound, I took it as a sign and I remained confident that the next real conversation I'd be having with my wife would be about circumcision. Or, perhaps, which position our son will play, shortstop or center field.[2]

When it finally came time to push, I was given the job of holding leg number two—a vital job that allowed me to be a part of this magical process while also leaving me one hand free to check e-mail and change my fantasy baseball lineup. I was also able to get updates on my softball team's progress that night. The score, according to one very reliable teammate, currently stood at 18 beers consumed (us) to 16 beers consumed (them), and the teams had a gentlemen's agreement to stop running to first base. I shared this good news with my wife, but she seemed disinterested for some reason. The doctor, on the other hand, offered up a high five.

Just then, the moment we had all been waiting for arrived: *The Wonder Years* marathon began on the delivery room television! But before I could catch a glimpse of my junior high crush, Winnie Cooper, the baby's head popped out. Then arms. Then a torso. Then butt. Then feet. The baby was covered in what I can only assume is the stuff used in lava lamps. He looked kind of like an alien, but he was here. My son was here.

"It's a girl!" the doctor said.

I passed out.

ACCEPTANCE (SORT OF)

I want to make this clear: From the minute you lay eyes on your daughter, you will be absolutely enamored with her and you'll be happy that you have a healthy baby girl.[3]

Outwardly, I was happy. Inwardly, I was extremely *scared*. I had played this moment over and over in my head at least a million times, and, in each scenario, labor didn't involve insurance-form

---

[2] Just kidding, the correct answer is clearly left-handed pitcher.
[3] Though a monkey would have been pretty cool, too.

papercuts or lava lamp goo. The birth was simple. A stork, whom I had named Marvin, would drop off a baby boy. I would put a baseball hat on that baby boy and name him Pete "The Hit King" Rose Klems, after legendary ballplayer and professional autographer Peter Edward Rose. I would be the envy of my friends. I would also later pay Pete Rose $50 to autograph Pete "The Hit King" Rose Klems's forearm.

But my wife, being completely unreasonable, would not allow me to name our daughter after Pete. Or Babe Ruth. Or anyone from the Transformers family, like Megatron.

"We have a daughter," she said. "Your daughter deserves a beautiful name, like Olivia or Nora."

Here is the first in a long line of valuable lessons you are going to learn throughout this book:

Dad Lesson

Your opinion on important matters (like which TV shows to watch) and lesser important matters (like baby names) doesn't matter anymore. If you're lucky, you can occasionally choose the pizza place you are ordering from—but even that is hit or miss. So, in order to avoid long, dragged-out fights that you will ultimately lose to a house full of women anyway, you must pick your battles wisely.

"I think we should stick with Megatron."

NAMING YOUR BABY GIRL BRACKETOLOGY-STYLE

Picking a baby name is a battle royale that resembles the NCAA March Madness basketball tournament. As parents, we are now members of an important selection committee who, after months and months of reading baby name books, studying the statistics, and checking to see which names lend themselves to the worst nicknames (Lydia Chlamydia), assemble a list of names vying to win over our hearts and become our baby's name.

The discussion will be spirited and filled with useful, constructive criticism like, "That is the dumbest name suggestion I've ever heard in my life." We rule out names of grade school bullies, ex-girlfriends, Hollywood socialites, names your parents have suggested, names often associated with dogs and, reluctantly, video game characters. (Sorry Princess Zelda; I made a play for you.) After a full season of debate, we finally settle on a mix of sixty-four girl names that both of us are willing to consider.

Like March Madness, there are perennial powerhouses that make it into the bracket year after year—like Elizabeth, Sarah, Mary, Kristin, Katie, Jennifer, and Jessica. These names carry prestige, have reputable histories and, most likely, are also the name of one of your family members who will believe you when you say, "Of course we named the kid after you because we love you so much." Though, in all likelihood, you probably named your daughter after Jessica Alba.

The new millennium has added a few newcomers to the brackets that now show up every year, like Madison and Emma. These names get points for being trendy and, somehow, lose points for being trendy. I actually don't understand the math in this equation. My wife tries to explain it, but my brain explodes. All I know is that the algorithm she uses only rules out names that *I* like.

Stupid math.

Next are bubble names, ones that have decent stats and just enough magic to crack the tournament, like Lynn and Melissa. These names held popularity for decades, but thanks to some recruiting violations and your mom having too many friends with these names, they're unlikely to make it past the Sweet 16.

Finally, you have your Cinderella stories—names that your wife never would have allowed into the bracket, but sneaked in via automatic bid because you asked her while she was half asleep. This is also known as "winning the conference tournament." It includes names you've always loved, like Violet and Bacon and Chiquita. Names you heavily root for that, occasionally, will make a deep run in the bracket. But rarely do these Cinderella teams win the whole thing because, well, your wife eventually wakes up. Still, it's good that they make the tournament because one day when your seventeen-year-old hates your guts because you won't let her see her favorite band, Rhymes With Truck, in concert, you can look her straight in the eye and say, "Your life could be worse. Your Mom tried to name you Chiquita."

This stage, as you may or may not know, is where the real excitement begins. The names are divided in half and seeded. Over the course of weeks, names will beat other names and winners will come forth. Some will be buzzerbeaters while others will be lopsided victories. Names you expect to go far will lose, and names that barely had a chance at first will make their way into the Elite 8. If you're lucky, by the time you make your way to the delivery room, you'll at least be down to the Final Four.

My wife and I had narrowed names down, but I wasn't paying close attention. Why would I? I don't pretend to be sick (cough, cough) and play hooky in March to watch the *women's* NCAA tournament. But our daughter deserved a name—a good one. (Yours does too.) It's the first chance you will have to keep her from becoming a stripper.

Choose wisely.

TEN DAUGHTER NAMES YOU SHOULD DEFINITELY CONSIDER

Still having trouble coming up with a name for your daughter? Unsatisfied with the name you picked? I've compiled a list of names that represent all the most important females we grew up with. These are names we've all considered as daughter names at one time or another. It's also very likely that after a long night of drinking in college with your buddies, you lost a bet that binds you into picking a name off this list.

Just tack your last name on to any one of these and you are good to go.

1. Princess Leia
2. Princess Peach
3. Daisy Duke
4. Posh Spice
5. Carmen Electra
6. Sweet Caroline
7. Bloody Mary
8. Catwoman
9. Winnie Cooper
10. Mrs. Butterworth

BONDING WITH YOUR FATHER-IN-LAW

Once your daughter has a name, she is a real person. This is the moment you become officially aware that you have a daughter. Up until now, you had been proceeding as if you had a boy. But you can't anymore. You don't have a boy, you have a girl. A tiny, precious little girl who will one day become a woman. And you know what happens to women? They grow boobs and get hounded by these evil, blood-sucking creatures also known as "boys." Worse yet, one day she'll be interested in them, too. No more daydreaming about a son. Your mission is clear. You must protect her, at all costs.

This mission to protect has one quick benefit: You immediately form a bond with your father-in-law and now completely understand why he doesn't like you. You're a boy! This was an unimportant fact for the eight years you dated his daughter, but now that *you* have a daughter, it's time to apologize.

Sir, I'm so sorry I charmed your daughter with my rugged good looks and complete and total awesomeness. If you ever feel inclined to take a swing at me, I will understand. Just please avoid my face and genital region—they don't like getting punched.

In an effort to prevent your daughter from ever mingling with boys, you ask your father-in-law for advice—after all, a boy once courted his daughter and, ultimately, convinced her to marry him. He even caused her to have a baby (what a lowlife!). Only now can you appreciate how angry your father-in-law must be. The first talk I had with my father-in-law after the birth of my eldest daughter revolved around this topic. Our conversation went something like this:

Me: "What happened?"

Father-In-Law: "I let her out of the house."

Me: "I'm never going to do that."

Father-In-Law: "Good. Because if you do, she'll just marry some bozo."

Me: "Did you just call me a . . . wait, I just got a text message. NO WAY! My friend says they are rereleasing *Star Wars* on Blue Ray with 1,200 extra minutes of never-before-seen footage of George Lucas eating a pizza! I must have this."

Father-In-Law: "Don't let her out of the house."

Dad Lesson

Tread carefully when taking advice from your father-in-law. Remember, he wasn't successful in stopping you.

IN THE END

Even though the day didn't go quite as planned, all in all, you survived it. Some would even say you thrived during it. None of those people were probably present, but over time, as you retell the story of your daughter's birth to others, you can tweak a few of the details (like how the baby almost slipped right out of your wife but you used your beer-league softball skills to swoop in and make a diving catch—yeah, *that's* how you ended up on the floor, not from passing out at the first sight of a needle), you will convince them of your heroism. This is called "making the story better."

Things are starting to look up. The doctor gives you and your wife permission to take this baby home, which is amazing considering there's nothing on your resume to suggest that you are at all capable of raising a human being, especially a girl. This gives you pause: Should you trust a doctor who is willing to let you—the guy who once did a keg stand and then dove into a bush naked—take a baby girl home and raise her? So you ask for more time in the hospital, say, three years, to give you time to study the nursing staff's procedures and read up on raising a girl.

Unfortunately insurance won't cover that (trust me, I tried).

At this point you grab your bags and your wife and head to the car. Then you run back and grab your daughter, whom you forgot. During the long walk from the room to the car, you look into her beautiful eyes and start to rationalize things with her. I mean, really, how different could raising a girl be to raising a boy? Heck, I could just raise you as if you WERE a boy! Yeah, that's it! Maybe, when it's just us, I will even call you Megatron.

You silly fool! You think your wife (and any other females in your life that have a credit card and an online account at "All the Girliest Stores in the Universe") will let you do that? Rookie mistake.

But we've all been there. I've been there. Everything changes the minute you leave the hospital and pull into your driveway. Like I said, labor isn't painful at all, but what happens over the next few months is.

It's about time you learned the truth about what lies ahead.

Chapter 2

The Pink Hangover

(AND HOW TO DRESS YOUR DAUGHTER)

There are only six things you can never have too much of: air, money, baby kisses, laughter, sex, and Nacho Cheese Doritos. Pink is not on that list. Once you have a daughter, though, it'll feel like it's the *only* thing on that list.

Up until this point in your life, you've probably never owned anything pink. In fact, it's likely that you weren't even sure that pink was an actual color. Pink, for all intents and purposes, didn't exist in your life and was just as mythical as the Loch Ness Monster or a stress-free mother-in-law.

But from the moment you announce to the world that your wife did, indeed, give birth to a little baby girl, the cold, harsh truth hits you square in the jelly beans: Pink *does* exist. And it's out to ruin your life.

THEY EVEN MAKE *THAT* IN PINK?

As word spreads that you have a daughter, the gifts come rolling in. Unfortunately, they are not anything practical, like a new barbeque-tool set or season tickets to your favorite sports team. You receive an assortment of items that have one thing, and only one thing, in common: Pink.

Pink bibs. Pink hats. Pink balloons. Pink diapers. Pink diaper bags. Pink burp cloths. Pink crib sheets. Pink teething rings. Pink Bumbos (whatever the hell those are). Pink strollers. Pink car seats. Pink bottles. Pink bouncy seats. Pink photo albums. Pink dresses. Pink pants. Pink shoes. Pink hairbows. Pink onesies that say silly things like "If you think I'm cute, you should see my dad," which is an obvious attempt to blind you from the fact that it's pink. And more.

All these evil people, previously known as "family" and "friends," will search every corner of the earth, from here to Belarus, until they have purchased all the pink in the world—so they can give it to you, as if they are doing you a favor.

"Oh my, aren't these little pink booties adorable!" says Aunt Phyllis. "I only had to take one plane, two busses, a pontoon boat, and high jump over a five-story building to find the one boutique in North America that sells them! Aren't you as excited as I am?! I could have instead put the $100 it cost me to get there and the $75 it cost for the shoes in her college fund, which will probably need to be filled at a clip of $17,000 a year to keep up with tuition growth and inflation, but these booties were too cute to pass up." (See Dad Lesson.)

Dad Lesson

Women are smart. Super smart. In fact, when raising your daughter, you will lean on your wife constantly because she's the resident expert in females (a subject you know nothing about). But when it comes to little baby girls' shoes, most women will absolutely lose their minds.

Thanks to Aunt Phyllis—and Aunt Debbie and Aunt Dale and Aunt Donna and Aunt Dannette and Aunt Martha and (not so surprisingly) Uncle Glenn—pink will soon be the only color left in your house. To emphasize just how much pink will overtake your life, I should use all-caps every time I write it just like this, PINK! But I won't, partially because I don't want to throw you into some sort of cataclysmic shock that could kill you and partially because my editor doesn't like it when I do that.

What Happened to Your Old Stuff?

Keep in mind that before you left for the hospital, your house was a normal mix of manly colors, ranging from blue to dark blue to even darker blue to midnight blue to taupe (which I think might be French for "blue"). Pictures of your favorite sports heroes lined the walls, wearing rough-and-tough uniforms that say things like "Bengals" and "Cowboys" and "The Jazz." The closest you ever came to harboring anything pink in your house were images of Paris Hilton in a swimsuit, whom your HDTV (named Stephen) *forced* you to watch. (Trust me, dude, I know. Your wife will think that *you* actually wanted to watch shows starring Paris Hilton, but we both know Stephen is to blame.)

When you return home, none of this still holds true (except for the Paris Hilton thing—shame on you, Stephen!). Pink, who apparently had one too many at the birth-celebration party, has thrown up all over your house. Everything you now own is pink. Your pictures of sports heroes are replaced by pictures of your daughter and she, of course, is wearing pink. No matter how hard you try to remove all the pink stuff and pull your posters and leg lamps and football-covered blankets out of the basement, it will be to no avail. Pink is everywhere, my friend.

Everywhere.

Worse yet—and I'm speaking from experience here—this pink hangover is going to last the rest of your life (or until you're lucky enough to be one of the 10 percent of males who go colorblind).

Pink Isn't Just a Color, It's a Lifestyle

It's not just the pink that will consume you, it's the fact that everything around you is changing. Your friends are treating you differently. Your television shows will eventually be replaced by girly cartoons. You can't even go to the bathroom—the one place in every house that you used to call your throne—without tripping over little pink shoes and pink-clothed dolls. Your pockets are not filled with wallets and keys, but with bows and barrettes that must remain on you at all times in case of an emergency.

Your manhood is not just being challenged, it's being squashed like the hopes and dreams of a *Saved by the Bell* reunion show (thanks a lot, Screech!). There's nothing you can do but watch and hope that one day your daughter grows up to like a few nonfeminine things, like baseball or musicals.

> ### Dad Lesson
>
> Don't wait for your daughter to demand a little masculinity, bring it to her. Make it a priority in her life. When your daughter gets a little older, say four years old, teach her a valuable skill set, like how to file your taxes or how to mercilessly boo Cubs fans. Your wife may look at you cross-eyed and try to whisk your daughter off to something less educational like "the park," without even considering the fact that the taxes are due in about an hour or that Cubs fans deserve it.[1]

THE FIVE STAGES OF GRIEF: HOW TO SURVIVE IN A PINK WORLD

In order to persevere through the onslaught of pink that is about to overtake your life, you have to think of pink as your new favorite sports team. For example, when someone buys your daughter a pink shirt, think of it as a jersey. To help with this, take every pink shirt she receives and add a number on the back. You can also add your last name. Or, if you prefer, use a clever pseudonym such as "My Dad Owns a Shotgun." I recommend continuing the practice until she is thirty.

Accepting the pink hangover is similar to facing the five stages of grief.

---

[1] If you are a Cubs fan and you purchased this book, know that I'm just kidding around. Some of my closest friends are Cubs fans. And if any of them have taken offense, from the bottom of my heart, I'm sorry.[2]

[2] I'm not sorry. Boo!

Stage #1: Denial and Isolation

"Not all girls *have* to wear pink. No child of mine would ever *like* such a repugnant hue, and I'm sure my daughter will be wise enough to choose a less awful favorite color, such as the lovely color puce (which I think is Italian for 'blue'). Perhaps she'll even start a war against pink and rebuke all the harm it's done to the world. At the very minimum, she can have the government outlaw its inclusion on men's ties."

Stage #2: Anger

"It's bad enough that I have to worry about future boys taking my daughter on future dates, I also have to put up with pink? What a load of bologna. What jerk invented the color pink anyway? I bet it was Simon Cowell. That guy is always inventing pure garbage."[3]

Stage #3: Bargaining

"Okay, she can wear pink on Mondays, Wednesdays, Fridays, and every other weekend. On non-pink-wearing days, she must be dressed in blue jeans and a gray hooded sweatshirt. When the temperature is above 85 degrees Fahrenheit and such heavy apparel is detrimental to comfort, it is acceptable to substitute a T-shirt for the hooded sweatshirt so long as it has a picture of me on it holding some sort of deadly weapon, like a sword or a rocket launcher."

Stage #4: Depression

"Why do you hate me, God???" *Uncontrollable sobbing* "Is it the porn? Is it all the X-rated porn? I swear I just watch it for the articles!"

---

[3] Simon Cowell: If you are reading this book 1) I'm starstruck and 2) forgive me. Pretend I never said anything and instead blame it all on Ryan Seacrest.

Stage #5: Acceptance

"I guess pink isn't *so* bad, especially when it's surrounding my daughter's beautiful little smile. I suppose it's possible I could even learn to like it. I suppose it's also possible that I could learn to like a Simon Cowell show. Hell, if I can tolerate pink, anything is possible!"

Getting through the Five Stages of Getting Used to Pink is only half the battle, though. The other half is medication. Lots and lots of medication. An occasional viewing of the Back to the Future trilogy doesn't hurt, either.

ARE OTHERS COLORBLIND?

Once you have moderately accepted the fact that you are not allowed to have any other favorite color than pink anymore, you start to embrace it a little bit. You proudly take your daughter places, like the grocery store or the bar that sponsors your softball team, and flaunt her pink as if it's a championship trophy celebrating that you have a daughter.

This will solicit a number of responses that will range from "Awwwwwwwww" to "Oh my, that's a lot of pink!" to "Seriously, chief, put some pants on."[4] But the one comment you'll get over and over and over again that sends chills down your spine is this one:

"What an adorable little *boy* you have there!"

Yes, yes, I . . . wait, what? Boy? *Boy?!* What do you mean, *boy?* This baby has so much pink on her that if you peeled her like a banana she'd still look like a unicorn.[5] What else could you

---

[4] This one usually happens during the first few weeks when sleep deprivation kicks in, causing you major embarrassment as you forget basic things, like putting on pants and switching Derek Jeter out of your fantasy baseball lineup when the Yankees have the day off. What happened to you, man? Seriously, what happened to you?

[5] Wait, are unicorns pink? I have no idea. Well, if not, insert something else in there that's pink like a big frilly tutu or the early stages of a sunburn.

possibly do? My wife suggested getting her ears pierced to prove to others once and for all that she was a girl, but this seemed like a terrible idea to me. Getting your ears pierced is the first step toward dating. My gut instincts, which are right nearly 11 percent of the time, tell me to hold off on getting her ears pierced until she's at least old enough to be president. And even then that may be jumping the gun a little.

I've racked my brain time and again, trying to figure out why people so readily mistake baby girls for baby boys. Maybe it's the fact that she looks scrappy or perhaps it's because she's balder than her old man (which is a tough bill to live up to these days), but my ultimate guess is that these people think *all* babies are boys. If you encounter one of these people who mistakes your daughter for a boy, your best bet is to ignore them and walk away.

But just before you do, sneakily drop a silent but deadly fart on them. Trust me, they deserved it.

SHE CAN'T JUST WEAR BASEBALL JERSEYS (SAYS YOUR WIFE)

Before you have a daughter, the only person you ever have to worry about dressing is yourself (if you already have a son—which I don't—I can only imagine that you don't have to worry about dressing him because he was born with innate survival skills such as dressing himself, hunting, and doing "the wave"). Picking out something to wear was quite simple: Grab the first articles of clothing you find, regardless of whether it matches, give it the sniff test to make sure it doesn't smell like feet, and slip it on. You never had to worry about not wearing something awesome because everything you owned *was* awesome. In fact, I'm confident that if I looked in your closet right now I'd find the perfect mix of sports jerseys, jeans, T-shirts you've worn since high school, long-sleeve tees you wear under the T-shirts you've worn since high school, and a set of collared Oxford shirts that you break out only for work, Christmas, and any other time your wife demands that you "look ~~less awesome~~ nice."[6]

Dad Lesson

Outfits typically match in color or in design, much like a baseball uniform. There's only one major drawback: When dressing your daughter, all the shirts, pants, and skirts you pull out of her dresser drawer will have no outward sign telling you which side is the front and which is the back. Occasionally there will be buttons, which you will always assume go in the back—but that's not true. They often go in the front. Sure, you could check for a tag, which indicates the back. And you could see if the top and bottom are made by the same brand, which helps match outfit pieces. But that's so time-consuming! This unequivocally proves that the person who invented outfits for little girls hates men. The solution? Prepare to apologize for putting your daughter's clothes on her backwards.

YET ANOTHER CHANGE

Things change dramatically once you have a daughter, mainly because moms and dads have completely different views on how to dress their daughters. Dads prefer to dress daughters like they dress themselves (grab the first thing, sniff test, etc). Moms, on the other hand, prefer to make sure their daughters are dressed in a cute ensemble of pretty colors, also known as an "outfit." In case you are unclear what an "outfit" is (like I was), I pulled the definition from Dictionary.com:

---

[6]Who are we kidding, you always look ~~awesome~~ nice.

Outfit: (noun) A set of usually matching or harmonious garments and accessories worn together; coordinated costume; ensemble: a new spring outfit.

Because I only understood three words in that sentence, I asked my wife to translate:

Outfit: (noun) The opposite of what you have picked out.

THERE'S THE PINK AGAIN

I didn't have the first clue on how to dress my first daughter when she was born. Her dresser overflowed with tons of outfits, all of which were pink. I know what you're thinking: If they are all pink, doesn't that mean they all match and can work as outfits no matter which combination you pull out? Oh, you silly fool! That's the kind of dumb common-sense thing that your wife uses to mock you behind your back to her closest friends.

"You'll never believe this, but my husband tried to put little Rosie in a pink pair of pajamas where the top half featured animals that are indigenous to *North* America while the bottom half had animals that are indigenous to *South* America! How embarrassing would that have been if someone visited us in the middle of the night, peeked into her room, and saw her sleeping dressed like that! Thank goodness little Rosie has me to save her from her dad's atrocious mistakes."

No matter how hard you try to dress your daughter in appropriate apparel, you will fail—miserably. This will lead to a disorder documented by the American Medical Association known as Dressing a Daughter Stress Syndrome (or DADSS). DADSS is especially common among new dads, and constantly makes us feel inadequate as parents. Symptoms include (but are not limited to):

- Insomnia
- Male-pattern baldness
- Excessive flatulence
- Missing key plays during the TV broadcast of your favorite sporting event
- Forgetting to take out the garbage
- Losing your ability to solve a Rubik's Cube
- The development of ear hair

The bad news is you'll probably experience all of these symptoms, sometimes at the same time. The good news is, it only lasts until your daughter is old enough to dress herself, which, hopefully, starts when she's six months old. But if you're like me and keep impregnating your wife with daughter after daughter after daughter, you'll suffer from DADSS for many, many years to come. And by then, the hair damage is done. Worse yet, as it falls out it's likely clogging your bathtub drain, necessitating costly plumber visits. (Ask if they have a DADSS discount—if that plumber has daughters, he probably does.)

USE WHAT YOU KNOW

Do you remember the scene in *The Karate Kid* where Mr. Miyagi teaches Daniel how to do bad-ass karate moves through the menial chore of waxing a car?[7] This got me thinking, *What if our moms had the foresight to teach us chore-based lessons that would subliminally help in our efforts to dress our future daughters?* I mean, our moms made us do countless chores when we were younger, all of which seemed pointless. Maybe a greater lesson hid within this work? Maybe our moms channeled Mr. Miyagi so we could defeat the

---

[7] Dude, if you don't know what I'm talking about then immediately put this book down, go to your local video store and rent it. You *totally* need to watch that movie.

evil forces of the Cobra Kai Dojo, er, I mean, successfully dress our daughter to the appeasement of our wives?

I decided to examine the four main chores my mom bestowed upon me in my younger years, looking closely to see if she secretly snuck in some sage-like wisdom.

Washing My Own Laundry

How I Was Taught: When I came home from college the first time, I spent all of eleven seconds at my parents' house—just enough time to hand my mom my dirty laundry. I was *shocked* to learn that she didn't appreciate this benevolent gesture (I thought this was our way of bonding!). The next time I came to town, she showed me how to separate my clothes into whites and colors, and to also use the washing machine and dryer (both of which were more complicated than hand-coding a website). Then she taught me how to fold clothes properly. Much to my surprise, it didn't involve throwing them on the floor.

Potential *Karate Kid*–Style Lesson on Dressing Daughters: Separating the clothes showed that we, as dads, need to separate the way we dress ourselves from the way we dress our baby girls, accounting for our differences. The washer and dryer are a metaphor for how difficult this will be for us to accept. And folding the clothes teaches us that, despite our best efforts, we will still ignore most of what we learn and pile her clothes next to our clothes on the floor.

Vacuuming the Carpet

How I Was Taught: My mom was very specific about this one: Use two hands and hold it tightly. Don't let it fall over. Replace or empty the bag of dirt when it's full.

Potential *Karate Kid*–Style Lesson on Dressing Daughters: I'm pretty sure those are the exact rules to changing a diaper, which is a pivotal step in dressing a daughter. If only it also taught you how to keep from getting baby poop on your sleeve.

Washing Dishes

How I Was Taught: One day my mom handed me a sponge and a plate. She showed me how to apply the proper amount of suds and water before scrubbing in a distinct circular motion. This was key for removing the thick layer of melted cheese that clung to the plate (we used cheese to mask the terrible flavor of all vegetables). From there it was on to the drying station where we unfolded a dishtowel and patted the plate gently so it dried without watermarks.

Potential *Karate Kid*–**Style Lesson on Dressing Daughters:** Before dressing your daughter, you must apply a layer of baby lotion to her body to avoid particular medical ailments such as her "skin drying out" or her "smelling funky." Learning how to wash dishes teaches us how to properly lotion up our baby daughters for the highest level of skin care possible. It also is a great lesson on how to, if the event calls for it, remove cheese from their skin.

Picking Out My Own Clothes

How I Was Taught: At a certain age my mother asked me to pick out my clothes, placing them on the side of my bed the night before I needed to wear them. I did this every day with great success. Though, in full disclosure, I went to Catholic school, so five out of seven days each week my only choice was a Catholic school uniform.

Potential *Karate Kid*–**Style Lesson on Dressing Daughters:** Just buy uniforms. Boy uniforms. This eliminates any chance of confusion or "mismatching" of clothes. It also has the side benefit of making our daughters tomboyish, making it less likely they'll ever want to do anything stupid like take ballet or date.

At the end of this examination, I concluded that my mom was a genius, teaching me all sorts of skills that are useful now that I have a daughter. I also concluded that I suck at all these skills in spite of my mom's best efforts.

DAUGHTER DRESSING NEEDS A POINT SYSTEM

Perhaps dads would excel at daughter dressing if there were a point system, like in sports, allowing us to track our progress and, more important, letting us compete with other dads. Points could be awarded as follows (and tracked by ESPN):

1 POINT FOR:
- Putting diaper on
- Putting diaper on facing the right way
- Remembering to fasten all three onesie snaps
- Putting on her socks

2 POINTS FOR:
- Picking clothes that actually fit her
- Putting her head through the shirt's head hole, not an arm hole

3 POINTS FOR:
- Picking out an outfit that matches
- Picking out an outfit that matches that doesn't include a sports jersey

10 POINTS FOR:
- Choosing weather-appropriate clothes (this point total comes at my wife's suggestion)

Then, just like at the end of *The Karate Kid*, there could be a tournament where dads who had accumulated the highest scores around the country competed on who dressed his daughter the best. Moms could serve as judges and award us different color belts based on our level of competence. The top winners of the tournament could net cool prizes, like a baseball signed by our favorite player or one month off diaper duty or a copy of this book! It could be glorious!

But alas, there is no Dressing Your Daughter competition. No point system. No awesome tournament where we can better ourselves as dads while also letting loose our raw competitive instincts. It's time to accept that there's absolutely no chance our skills in this arena will ever improve. So unless your mom is available to come over whenever it's your turn to dress little Rosie, you'll need the following cheat-sheet.

THE SEVENTEEN RULES EVERY DAD MUST KNOW WHEN DRESSING HIS DAUGHTER

When I first started dressing my eldest daughter, I thought to myself, *Dressing a girl shouldn't be this difficult, right? Slap some jeans and a Cincinnati Reds jersey on her and she should be good to go!*

I asked my own dad, a wise man in his own right, how he coped with dressing my younger sister. He thought about this for a few minutes, then spoke with the authoritative voice I'd grown accustomed to over the years.

"Son," he said, "I abided by the two rules I used to dress myself: One article must have a neck-hole and the other must cover the crotch."

Two rules. Simple. Easy to remember. Kept you from violating any state laws. I liked it.

My wife, on the other hand, has a full seventeen rules for dressing our daughters. They are complicated, confusing, and intimidating. (They are also endorsed by every other woman I've ever met.) These rules were not pulled out of a hat—though, to any normal human being who isn't a female, they might look that way. The basics were crafted centuries ago and have been adapted by each generation of wife/mother. While slight details may change from household to household, the essence of each rule is intact.

But let's be honest: seventeen rules are too many for any dad to remember; after all, dads' minds are only programmed to retain things like baseball statistics, what-beats-what in poker, and which flavor of snow cone is the best (lemon-lime). Even Einstein couldn't remember his wife's set of rules for dressing their daughter. And if he—father of e=mc²—couldn't do it, how could women expect us regular dads—who don't even know what e=mc² means—to cope with so many rules?

In order to avoid future problems, I wrote the rules down on a little cheat sheet that I keep hidden in the top dresser drawer of each daughter's bedroom. I reference it every morning and recommend that you do too. Since I started doing this, my wife and I stopped fighting about clothing, which has opened up some valuable free time that we now dedicate to fighting about the societal value of the "I'm So Excited" episode of *Saved by the Bell*. (And yes, there totally is some.)

So, without further ado, here are the Seventeen Rules Every Dad Must Know When Dressing His Daughter:

1. Clothes need to match—in color and style, *and* in "type of animal on them."
2. Diapers must go on under tights, not over.
3. A shirt with a ketchup stain does not "have red in it."
4. No matter how you dice it, vertical stripes on a shirt do not match horizontal stripes on pants.
5. Shorts are not a year-round option.
6. No socks with sandals (this rule also applies to dressing dad).
7. Bowls are not hats.
8. Pants are not hats.
9. Underwear are not . . . you get the picture.

10. Adam committed original sin when he ate the apple. His second sin was dressing his daughter in white after Labor Day.
11. Siblings in matching outfits are cute. Dad and daughters in matching Megadeth tees are not.
12. Changing from PJs into another set of PJs is not "dressing her."
13. Wristbands are not "part of an outfit."
14. If she wears her Joey Votto baseball jersey on Monday, she can't wear it again for at least ten business days.
15. She also can't wear the other eleven jerseys you bought her for the duration of those ten business days.
16. Grunge is dead. So are you if you dress your baby in it.
17. And finally . . . if you have to sniff it, it's off limits.

There you have it. The list of rules every father must have. Print it out. Tuck it away under your daughter's 204 pairs of socks. Hang it from the ceiling like a mobile. Wear it on one of those laminated forearm bands that quarterbacks use to keep track of plays. Do whatever you have to do to keep it close, even if that means printing off a copy and keeping it in every room of the house. It's one of the most valuable resources that exists in the universe (way more valuable than $e=mc^2$) and, if you abide by it religiously, you will not only cut back on the number of fights you have with your wife, but you'll also cut back on the number of times she calls you a "bozo" in front of all her girlfriends. This is good, because the more her girlfriends like you, the more attractive you become to them. And the more attractive you become to them, the more attractive you become to your wife.

Which you need, considering there's probably baby poop on your sleeve.

Chapter 3

Your
Social Life

(RIP)

Right up until your wife gave birth, you probably had a healthy social life. Maybe you went out for drinks with coworkers after a long day at the office, played in a local softball league, or marked fantasy football draft night on your calendar months in advance. Well, all of that has now changed. After all, when you become a father, you have new responsibilities, new time constraints, and new financial goals (see Chapter 13). You also will learn that the term "all-nighter" has an entirely different meaning.

Your nonparent friends will *try* to understand. When your daughter is born, you'll receive so many "congratulations" and pats on the back that you'll develop a mild case of scoliosis. (In fact, I've been told that chiropractors scour the birth announcements for potential clients.) When you have a son, they might also hand you a cigar. When you have a daughter, the best they can muster is a side-to-side shake of the head. That side-to-side head shake is code for, "Whoa, buddy, you've got your work cut out for you, especially in those teenage years."

You're trying to survive the first few weeks and people are already thinking about teenage years? Are they insane?

AT FIRST . . .

Your friends might try to comfort you by giving your daughter baseball gloves and footballs anyway (all of which will be pink, as you learned in the previous chapter) to let you know that even though your daughter is, technically, a girl, it doesn't mean she can't enjoy some of the more masculine activities you love. (Sure, she'll never be able to appreciate a good bathroom sword fight or challenge you to a mustache-growing competition,[1] but it's certainly possible that one day she'll tear up with you at the end of

---

[1] If she can battle you in a mustache competition, be afraid. Be very afraid.

Field of Dreams.[2]) They may even try to call her by initials, like "EJ" or "AJ," in an attempt to sound less girly and ease your transition into fatherhood of a daughter, and work around her bedtime when scheduling fantasy drafts.

But when you have to skip meeting them for the first day of March Madness because your daughter has a "fever" of 98.7, off come the gloves. Once the "You are going to have to protect your daughter from guys like us" jokes wear off, folks start chiming in on your own manliness. They ask if you need help satisfying your wife. They might buy you fruity drinks with tiny umbrellas in them (which you secretly love but can't admit in public unless you *really* want to be shamed). They start calling you by girls' names like "Nancy" or "Nancy," indicating that they are not really that clever. My personal favorite is when they refer to you by your wife's maiden name, as if that will somehow get under your skin and eat at you.

(It totally gets under your skin and eats at you.)

But no matter what they call you, it doesn't compare to the conception conversations you have to endure, all of which, go something like this:

"So you and your wife did the horizontal mambo and you impregnated her with a girl?"
"Please don't ever use the phrase 'horizontal mambo' again."

"Couldn't seal the deal for a boy, eh?"
"Seal the deal?"
"Don't you have any male swimmers in there?"
"I'm not having this conversation with you."

"Come to think of it, you are pretty girly. I bet you can't even name an Arnold Schwarzenegger movie."

---

[2] I tear up just thinking about the father and son game of catch at the end. Please turn away for a moment.

"Terminator. Total Recall. The Running Man. Kindergarten Cop . . ."
"You probably don't even know who Arnold Schwarzenegger is."
"Can you even spell 'Schwarzenegger'?"

"I bet this happened because you watch *Glee.*"
"Shut up." (*Glee* is awesome.)

Once they finish that line of humor, they'll delve into their latest conquests with the ladies, recount your friend's crazy bachelor party in Vegas last week, and ponder whether they should sleep until 10 A.M. or 2 P.M. this Saturday (the correct answer is 4 P.M.). Face it: their life is different than from now. Your social life as you once knew and loved it is over.

THE EIGHT CHALLENGES OF SHEER MANLINESS

At some point, you won't be able to take it any longer. You'll hear a story about an epic night you missed out on because you were "sleep training" your angel. You'll look longingly at your buddy's apartment, which is completely devoid of anything pink. You'll snap. This is the moment you must challenge these friends to a testosterone-filled duel. You can't let your manliness get insulted like that; you're still a guy, even though you're a father now. Sure, you can't jet off to Vegas at a moment's notice or spend the entire weekend crushing your friends in a video game tournament, but that doesn't mean you're completely lame.[3]

Plus, what kind of example would you be setting for your daughter if you didn't defend yourself? You want her to know that you are strong and can protect her. Of course, you are hopped up on so much Mountain Dew to mask the fact that you are super

---

[3] I don't care what our wives say, video game tournaments are not lame.

sleep-deprived from having a newborn, you've been walking around challenging everything to a duel, including your wife, your mother, the kids across the street, and a lamppost.

When two men feel their manliness has been challenged, there are only eight acceptable ways to settle it. They are known as the Eight Challenges of Sheer Manliness (I've included the rules to help guide you):

Warm Beer Chugging

Call all your friends and find the one (there's always one) who has a case of beer that's been sitting in his garage for who knows how long. It's been through season after season, suffering through cold snaps and heat waves. Until now, those beers were considered lost soldiers. Open them up and chug one warm, stale beer after another. Truthfully, there are no "real" winners in this Challenge of Sheer Manliness. But the last man left standing without vomit on him technically walks away with the crown.

Paintball of Power

Both manly contestants start 100 feet apart. Each get one shot, then both must move forward one foot. Each take another shot and then move forward one more foot, and so on, until both players are close enough to make out. Person with the most paint marks on his clothing loses. If it's a tie, both players are placed ten feet apart and, on the count of three, begin shooting at each other's man parts until one player gives up.

Grill Off!

Big hunks of meat, two grills, one winner. The goal is to create the tastiest meal you can out of only beef and pork products. Acceptable items include burgers, steaks, hot dogs, bratwursts, mettwursts, anything with "wursts" on the end of it, pork chops, ribs, and wings. Remember: The only condiment allowed under the Manliness Challenge Bylaws is bacon (no, that is not a typo). This competition will prove to be the most popular with the rest of your buddies, who preside as judges.

Star Wars Trivia

Who is the only non-Jedi in the original Star Wars trilogy to use a lightsaber? In what language does "Vader" mean "father"? If you can answer these questions and more, you may be able to hang in a mano-a-mano battle of Star Wars knowledge. First dude to answer at least ten questions correctly wins. This may be the manliest of all the competitions. It's also the one least likely to impress your wife.[4]

Batting Cage Beatdown

Find a batting cage with a pitching machine that throws a minimum of ninety miles per hour. If you can't find one, bribe the worker to pump up one of the machines to hit that number. Each dude gets fifteen swings per round. First one to make contact (with the bat, not your body) wins. Helmets, cups, and an Iron Man body suit are highly recommended.

Bar Game Olympics

Like drinking? Like pool, darts, and foosball? Like the way your clothes stink after hours at your local watering hole? Then the Bar Game Olympics are for you. Play a round of each sport mentioned above, doing a shot every fifteen minutes. Best two out of three wins—or last man standing, whichever comes first.

Feats of Strength

Every member of your group of friends writes some sort of physical challenge on a piece a paper and drops it in a hat. Could be climbing

---

[4]The other least likely ways to impress your wife include: showing her your jorts collection, shaving a letter into your chest hair to help your buddies spell out your favorite sports team's name, playing "The Star-Spangled Banner" in armpit farts, and buying a ferret.

a tree. Could be arm-wrestling. Could be removing giant rocks from a friend's backyard so he can put in a swimming pool (seriously, if one of your asshole friends puts this in the hat you have my permission to elbow him in the groin—that said, you still have to complete the challenge, per the Manliness Challenge Bylaws.) You each pick one challenge out of the hat and both have to compete in each.

Grass-Cutting Faceoff

What better way to settle the score than a battle of the manicured lawns? You're scored in three categories: Speed, precision, and finesse. The best judges of this competition are your dad and your buddies' dads. They not only have the most experience in this area but will most certainly be overly critical. Get bonus points for sculpting a pattern, design, or your favorite sports team's logo into your yard.

Who Won?

Whether you win or lose, you send a message to all your friends that jokes about your lack of an acceptable social life will no longer be tolerated. They will ignore this message and continue to jab at you, of course, but at least you will feel better about yourself knowing you put up a good fight.

Also, by participating in this challenge, you've proved you have the guts and determination to stand up for not only yourself but for your daughter too. This is an important step is becoming a great dad. It's also a necessary step because one day your daughter will take interest in a boy and you will need every ounce of manliness you can muster to scare him off forever. (But we'll get to that later.)

THE OTHER GUY WITH A DAUGHTER

No matter how alone you may feel, remember that you're not. Someone else in your life, perhaps an old high school buddy or a member of your softball team, has a daughter. You just have to be able to spot him.

For example, at the end of your dugout bench, there's one guy on the team who isn't sticking it to you. It's not because he's kinder than the rest of your friends. It's because this gent is the only other guy on the team who has a daughter. You'll notice he looks worn and beat up. He's also much balder than you remember him being at the beginning of the season, which is a clear sign that his wife is pregnant again and, while he hasn't told anyone, he knows they are having another girl. He will not come to your defense when you need it most, but he will quietly take you aside and give you a hug.

Dad Lesson

Dads who have daughters don't *actually* hug other dads who have daughters—that would be weird. Instead, there is a secret handshake that was created back in A.D. 300 by an underground tribe of men known as the "Tony Danzas" who had daughters but didn't want their caveman buddies to know about it. I'm going to teach you the secret handshake right now:

High five, swing it down to a low five, fist-bump, explode the fist bump, forehead slap, tear down the cheek.

This friend has been dying for someone else to join his club and now he has you. Be prepared to receive Evites every weekend, asking if you and your daughter want to join him and his daughter at his house for an afternoon of watching the kids lie on the floor and do nothing. After all, this is, realistically, your social life now. He may be able to offer you some practical advice on how to apply butt cream to clear up a rash, but you will immediately become uncomfortable when you realize he's not talking about the baby.

Don't shake your head too much at him. He's been through a lot (remember, he's adjusting to having a daughter too). If anything, be sympathetic. One day you may need a little compassion after offering up butt-cream application advice to someone else.

GUY WHO WATCHES HOW YOU HANDLE IT

The only guy friend you have left who hasn't given you too much grief is the one considering having kids. He and his wife have been married so long that they have dust on them. There's no way he'd ever start a family without doing his due diligence and, for the past year, he's relied on you for help. When you announced your pregnancy, he paid close attention, charting everything in your life—from how you dealt with your wife's morning sickness to how you handled her mood swings to how many minutes you showered each day.[5] He's created diagrams and matrices and bar graphs and pie charts and sub-pie charts and pumpkin pie charts. He measured your batting average and slugging percentage all nine months to see which months your numbers spiked and which months they dipped, hoping to find some sort of correlation. (Correlation for what? I have no idea. But this guy earned a 4.0 in college and is known as "the brainy one" of your friends, so it's safe to assume that whatever he's correlating must be pretty boring.)

Once your baby has arrived, he continues to study your moves for months, bringing you food twice a week. The best part is he gets to watch how you cuddle with that adorable daughter of yours, holding her close, kissing her on the cheek, and snoozing with her on the couch for what can only be considered a thin slice of heaven. This seals the deal: He's definitely not having kids.

---

[5]Admittedly, that was pretty weird.

CLOWNING AROUND IS PART OF THE GAME

In the end, you'll be thankful for all your buddies and their jokes. When push comes to shove, they'll be there for you when you need it most.[6] Well, maybe not when you need it most. I mean, they won't exactly jump through hoops to help you change a dirty diaper or come over in the middle of the night to calm your daughter when she's screaming at decibel levels so loud you get ticketed for breaking the neighborhood noise ordinance. But, quite honestly, would you do that for them? Oh . . . you would? Um . . . you're kind of killing my point here.

The *point* is that they *will* offer to get you out of the house from time to time and buy you a beer at your favorite bar—maybe even two if it's happy hour. And they *will* treat your daughter nicer than they treat their own moms. And, from day one, they will make her feel welcome and part of the team.

That's because through thick and thin, these are the greatest group of guys you've known. They've been there for you your whole life and they will always come through in the clutch for you, even when—no, *especially* when—you have a daughter.

Though it could also be because the coed team is becoming a bit thin on girls and they need to stay in your good graces in order to convince you to let your daughter play the minute she is big enough to hold a bat. Either way, consider yourself lucky.

---

[6]Did that just rhyme? I didn't mean it to, but if so, you can now tell your wife that you've started reading poetry. Chicks dig that. (You're welcome.)

Chapter 4

Disney Is Going to Ruin Your Life

(COMMENCE OPERATION PRINCESS OVERLOAD)

By now, I think you are coming to the full realization that everyone is conspiring against you. Your family members, your friends, even the lady you see every week in church who tells you how she had two daughters, both of whom have left the religious life to go into the Godless career of wind surfing.

Church lady: "You better watch those daughters of yours and raise them right. Or else they are liable to get into something worse than wind surfing."
Me: "Like accounting?"
Church lady: "Like orgies."
Me: "I am never letting them out of my sight. Ever."

When you want your daughter to grow up well, you turn to the person whom you trust and respect more than anyone, whom you know shares the same Judeo-Christian values as you do and who only wants the best for your kids. That person is Walt Disney.

For your daughter's first couple of years, Disney is your friend. He posts messages on your Facebook page to celebrate your birthday. He retweets your funny hashtags, such as #100ReasonsBaconIsAwesome and #JustinTimberlakeSmellsLikeFarts. He lets you sing some of his best songs, like "When You Wish Upon a Star" and "Can You Feel the Love Tonight (Tonight)?" to your daughter to get her to fall asleep on your shoulder—and he doesn't even care that you're off key and that you mess up 50 percent of the lyrics.

Eventually, though, Disney turns on you. Disney unfriends you on Facebook. He tells your mother-in-law that you actually like it when she offers unsolicited parenting advice. He unleashes his evil plan to completely dominate your life with reckless (and expensive) abandon. This phenomenon is explained by a few simple algorithms that were developed by MIT mathematicians, who not only have doctorate degrees but also have daughters:

$$\text{Daughters} - \text{Disney} = \text{Grumpy}$$
$$\text{Dads} + (\text{Daughters} - \text{Disney}) = \text{No Sleepy}$$
$$\text{No Sleepy} + \text{Dads} + (\text{Daughters} - \text{Disney}) = \text{Dopey}$$
$$(\text{Dopey} + \text{Dads}) + (\text{Daughters} - \text{Disney}) = \text{Armageddon}$$
$$\text{Armageddon} = \text{Original name for Doc}$$

Therefore:

$$\text{Dads} + \text{Daughters} + \text{Disney} = \text{Happy}$$

(In academia, these algorithms are commonly referred to as "The Disney Dwarf Equations.")

Based on these very complex mathematical calculations, one thing is clear: When you have a daughter, Disney will come knocking on your door. Answer it, if you value your life.

THE FIRST SIGN DISNEY IS RUINING YOUR LIFE: PRINCESSES, PRINCESSES, AND MORE PRINCESSES

Once upon a time, your daughter will be tiny and full of potential. She'll have the ability to do anything she wants, including run for president or, even more impressive, play shortstop in the majors. Thanks to Disney, though, that potential will be harnessed and aimed at completing one mission: finding a prince.

Before Disney movies came into our lives, my daughters didn't care about boys at all. In fact, they generally ignored them (a father's dream!) and congregated with all the other girls to do fun things like hopscotch and drawing on our couch with permanent marker. They had dreams of being artists and doctors and puppeteers, which all died a painful death when we watched our first Disney movie.

It's not like there are Disney movies about princesses who want to grow up to be doctors or engineers. The plot of nearly every Disney movie is that the princess is saved by a prince (or a guy who has a lot of prince-ish qualities, like handsomeness) and then they fall in love and get married. What bologna. It's plots like this that cause me to have conversations like this:

"Dad?"

"Yes, sweetie?"

"I think I need to find myself a prince."

"You don't need a prince."

"Yes, I do!"

"Trust me, you don't."

"But Cinderella needed a prince."

"Cinderella also talked to mice. If you ask me, she had a screw or two loose."

"But I want a prince."

"Why?"

"To rescue me!"

"From what? A house full of toys and a mom who lets you eat ice cream way more than she should?"

"No, no. I love those things. To rescue me from evil people."

"How many evil people do you know?"

"There's the evil stepmom in *Cinderella*, the evil witch in *The Little Mermaid* . . ."

"I see. Can't I protect you from them?"

"No, dad, you can't."

"Why not?"

"Because you're not a prince."

"How do you know?"

"Because I asked mom what you were."

"What did mom say?"

"She said you're 'Italian.'"

With logic like that, who's to argue?

THE SECOND SIGN DISNEY IS RUINING YOUR LIFE: HALLOWEEN ISN'T SCARY ANYMORE

Thanks to Disney, Halloween is not scary anymore. It's true. Nearly every little girl under the age of nine (including yours) will turn down the chance to dress as something spooky, like a witch or a ghost or your mother-in-law, and instead will choose to be something sweet and sparkly, like Cinderella, Sleeping Beauty, Rapunzel, or any one of the other 12 million Disney princesses.

It took me a few years to come to this realization, so hopefully this information finds you before you lug all eleven boxes of Halloween decorations and costumes up from your basement. Also, you will need to invest in eleven more boxes to store all of the princess outfits you'll be conned into buying.

When I asked each one of my girls what they wanted to be for our most recent Halloween, they responded as follows:

Daughter #1: "SNOW WHITE!"

Daughter #2: "TINKERBELL!"

Daughter #3: "BLUB-ER-GUP!" (which is five-month-old speak for "THE LITTLE MERMAID!")

A son wouldn't choose to be a princess on the most creepiest day of the year. He'd be something scary with face paint and evil laughs. Something that would give you the goosebumps each time he jumped out from behind the couch and yelled, "BOO!" My girls, on the other hand, with their beautiful dresses, necklaces, and tiaras, were about as scary as a rainbow. At the rate we are going, I wouldn't be surprised if, in the coming years, one of them wanted to dress up as a hug.

Now before you completely give up on the holiday, let me tell you a little story.

I decided to fight Disney and try to take back Halloween. I made it my mission to add a little bit of scariness to our festivities by having "The Inaugural Klems Family Scary Mask–Making Night." I made sure to load up on supplies: paper grocery bags, crayons, markers, construction paper, pipe cleaners, bacon (to feast on), paint, and anything else around the house that we could find that wouldn't cause my wife to yell at us.

I planned to show the girls how fun being scary can be and had a full plan to scare my wife.

I waited until a night when she was out on the town, likely binge drinking with someone much handsomer than me,[1] and I went to work. I cleared out the furniture and organized crafty supplies all over the living room floor. I called my daughters, who were busy discussing the intricacies of making fake tea, and had them join me.

"Let's make some scary, scary masks and then surprise Mom when she gets home. WHO'S WITH ME?"

"WE ARE!" they all shouted, except for the baby, who farted in agreement.

I let them get to work. I offered to help with whatever they wanted. I cut out eyeholes. I cut out big, scary teeth to tape to the front of the paper bags. But then Ella, my four-year-old, stopped me.

"Dad, I don't want to put *those* teeth on my mask."

"Okay, hon, what do you want me to cut out for you? A giant creepy red tongue? Some brown, dirty teeth? A black-and-blue eyeball that looks like it's getting CHEWED?"

"Can you cut a pretty smile out of this pink construction paper?"

Long pause.

"Well, dear, that's not quite what I had in mind when I said we were making . . ."

"And can you twist these purple and pink pipe cleaners into arms and hands so I can still hug Mommy when I'm wearing the mask?"

Another long pause.

---

[1]Okay, this is obviously not true. There's no one handsomer than me.

"But your goal isn't to hug Mom when she gets home, it's to scare her."

"Don't worry, Dad, we're still going to yell 'BOO!'"

And with that she took two more paper bags, put them on her feet and started referring to them as her "glass slippers." I considered this strike one.

So I turned to my two-year-old and asked her if she made a scary mask.

"Daddy, my mask is *really* scary."

"That's GREAT! I'm so excited. Are those red blobs on your mask blood oozing out?"

"No Daddy, those are hearts. And over here I drew a unicorn."

Strike two.

I wanted to shake my head in disgust. These girls were not only soft, but they were waving their softness in my face like a badge of honor. And unless you have a fear of pink or suffer from uni-cornaphobia,[2] you will be able to walk through my house without spotting a single scary thing (unless you count the number of New Kids on the Block albums that my wife still currently owns).

Just as I thought the night was a total bust, my wife came home from painting the town red.[3] My pink, purple, and heart-covered monsters quickly put on their masks and hid behind the couch. As my wife walked into the room, they jumped and yelled "BOOOOOO!" and erupted with laughter. I'd like to think my wife was a little scared. She probably was, though it likely had less to do with the masks and more to do with the mess of construction paper, tape, and stickers that we'd forgotten to clean up, which were covering every last inch of our living room floor.

Strike three.

Maybe I can blame Disney for that too.

---

[2] The fear of unicorns.

[3] "Painting the town red" is actually a euphemism for "helping out at a local homeless shelter." And "helping out at a local homeless shelter" is actually a euphemism for "shopping."

THE THIRD SIGN DISNEY IS RUINING YOUR LIFE: BOARD GAMES

Fatherhood is about taking risks and teaching your daughter life lessons, like how to be a respectful winner and how to be graceful when you don't win. I learned these lessons growing up while playing board games with my mom and dad. It was one of my favorite things to do. It didn't matter what the game involved, so long as it had a board or dice or cards or a Hungry Hungry Hippo. I played it until my parents made me go to bed—and even then I'd lie awake in bed, dreaming about playing board games. I also dreamt about Alicia Silverstone. Oh yeah, that's right. In my dreams, the two of us would play Scrabble until the wee hours of the morning. Talk about an awesome fantasy.

The Benefits of Competition

My wife isn't much of a game player. Luckily, one of the bright spots of having kids is that they typically are. Each of my daughters showed an interest in playing games from a very early age. From peek-a-boo to hide-and-seek to "Who Can Drive Mom Crazy First by Making the Loudest, Most Obnoxious Noise," they all had a knack for healthy competition. I figure if I could teach my daughters how to dominate games, they will use those skills to dominate other things in life, such as school, softball, and "Who Loves Her Dad the Most" competitions. As far as I'm concerned, the sooner I could get my daughters started, the better.

Games today aren't quite like games were when you and I were kids. The traditional boards of yesteryear have been replaced by princesses. And the pieces used to move around the boards have been replaced by princesses. And the group of kids you used to play against and poke fun at have now been replaced by princesses (that's right, your daughter and her friends will likely get dressed up in beautiful dresses and crowns before sitting down to play with you).

They're Even on Board Games!?

Yes, my friends, Disney has sneaked its way into every board game imaginable.

Let me give you an example. For my middle daughter's second birthday, a family member gave us Yahtzee. Yahtzee is a game that I played exclusively from second grade through junior high because I loved it so much. It gave me a natural high to enjoy the luck involved with the roll of the dice combined with the skill of predicting where to play your worst rolls to minimize overall damage and build the highest score possible. My mom loved the game too, not only because it taught me math, but also because it kept me entertained for hours. Few pieces were needed to play and you could start a game nearly anywhere.

So when my daughter opened the present, I jumped for joy!

"About time we started playing some board games around this house," I said.

As I looked more closely at the box though, I realized this wasn't the traditional Yahtzee I'd grown accustomed to playing. This was some sort of special Princess Yahtzee. It involved a board, not a scorepad. Every player receives six cards, each with the face of a different princess on it (think baseball cards only smaller, less collectable, and without stats on the back). The sides of the dice displayed no numbers. Once again, pictures of Disney princesses covered each die. You no longer attempt to get challenging combinations such as a large straight or a full house. Now your only job is to get as many of the same princesses as possible in the allotted three rolls (or however many rolls your daughter chooses to take). Plus, you will find yourself saying things that would *appall* the younger, Yahtzee-loving version of you.

- Four Sleeping Beauties? Nice!
- Five *Aladdin*'s Jasmine? That's a Yahtzee (I think)!
- Well, no, hon, you can't keep that die because it landed on Snow White and she's your favorite.
- If you *really* want to make the cards dance like they are at the grand ball we can, but I'd really like to keep playing the game.
- You're tired of this game and want to play something else? Perfect! Wait, you want to play Disney Princess Monopoly?
- No, we are not adding a princess tower to the house.
- Yes, I will wear a princess crown too. Please don't tell your mother.

And so on. The initial shock can leave you paralyzed. It can also make you do crazy things, like search online for hours until you find a vintage version of the game, just like the one you used to play, and then bid way too much for it. (Remember, it's likely you are competing with other dads who have daughters and are also stuck playing nothing but princess versions of the games too. They are just as desperate as you, so the bidding gets expensive. I'm not trying to deter you. On the contrary—I'm just letting you know that the overtime hours you put in and that second job you acquire to help pay off the debt of buying these games is totally worth it.[4] Also, any money left over from that additional work will come in handy when paying for your daughter's future wedding (but we'll get to that later).

The only way to enjoy these games is to remember that years from now, when your daughter is grown and married and has a daughter of her own, your granddaughter will want to play these Disney princess games too. Over and over and over again. And this will be the perfect punishment for that clown who married your daughter.

Dad Lesson

When you have a daughter, everyone (including your grandmother) will ask you the annoying question, "When are you taking her to Disney World?" The correct answer is: "I'm going to punch you in the face." This is an idle threat, of course, because you'd never punch your grandmother in the face (unless she really, really deserved it), but if you wave your fist, furrow your brow, and look mean and scary when you say it, they'll ask you less often.

WHY YOU WILL EVENTUALLY FORGIVE DISNEY

The truth is, if you love your daughter and care for her and teach her how to properly slide into second base feet-first, you will be her Disney prince (and, in my case, an Italian one). For always and forever. You're the one she'll turn to when she scrapes her

---

[4]Not because your daughter will play the game with you, because she won't. After all, there are no princesses in it. The value is being able to resell it online to another desperate dad for a nice profit. The key is putting it up just after Christmas—that's when most dads are playing the princess versions for the first time and begin to lose their minds.

knee. You're the one she'll call when she needs help with her math homework. You're the one whose shoulder she'll cry on when that first boy breaks her heart (and you'll also be the one to punish him for that by starting a rumor that he has superherpes).

Disney is going to knock the wind out of you time and time again, but it's your job as that sweet little girl's father to suck it up, brush it off, and guide her as best as you can. Let her know that you hope she finds a prince one day (only after she turns thirty and with your approval, of course), but that she doesn't need a prince to define her. And that you love how beautiful she looks as a princess, but that you also love it when she wears facepaint and talks like a pirate. And that you'll always play games with her, even if that means five Snow Whites makes a Yahtzee.

In the end, we'll probably be thanking Disney for helping us create such wonderful memories with our daughters. Disney will likely thank us too. Mainly because we've spent nearly 89.6 percent of our annual adjusted gross income with them, but also because our daughters will hopefully inspire a new generation of Disney creators to make princesses who are strong willed, self-sufficient, and brave.

Though if they still choose to dress them in glass slippers, I won't complain.

Chapter 5

The Dora Years

(COME ON, VAMANOS!)

Until about the age of eighteen months, your daughter will let you watch anything on TV. Doesn't matter what you flip on the tube, she'll turn her cheek to it and focus on something a lot less interesting, like a Cheerio that's been hiding under the couch for God knows how long, or a mound of dirty clothes you've piled in the corner. In fact, she's more agreeable than your wife, who claims that the maximum times a person *should* watch *SportsCenter* in a day is once. This is ridiculous, of course. You and I both know that there is no maximum to how many times a person should watch *SportsCenter* in a day. There is a minimum though, and it is eleven.

Sometime between the ages of eighteen months and two years old, the dynamics change. Your daughter no longer looks the other way on breezy fall weekends when you attempt to watch thirty-six consecutive hours of football, and she stops falling for the "I've Got Your Nose" routine that kept her confused and entertained (and a little scared) for however long you needed to get through the fourth quarter. She's either given up on that Cheerio or realized that she can get fresh ones by opening the pantry door.[1] She stops all your attempts to distract her and suddenly develops something that you've been trying to thwart since her birth: An opinion.

"Ready to watch some sports with daddy?" you ask.

"Dora!"

"Huh?"

"Dora!"

"I've got your nose!"

"DORA!"

"But it's the bottom of the ninth ..."

"DORA! DORA! DORA!"

"Are you sure you won't consider ..."

"DORA! DORA! DORA! DORA! DORA!"

---

[1]Remember how you spent $10 on that childproof doorknob protector and the only one in the family who can't open it is you? Money well spent, my friend. Money well spent.

Keep in mind this is fairly impressive because the only other two words she knows are *mama* and *dog*, though in full disclosure, she points to you when referring to both. But hey, she uses Dora in the correct context! The downside, though, is that your rule over the TV has come to an end. By the time you get it back, most of your favorite athletes will probably be retired and *The Simpsons* will have completed their fifty-eighth season on FOX.

At this point you have two choices: You can turn on *Dora the Explorer*, your daughter's new BFF, or you can watch as she throws the remote directly through the center of your 50-inch high-definition television. The choice is yours.

Choose wisely. Choose Dora.

WHAT YOU NEED TO KNOW ABOUT DORA

Dora the Explorer is a seven-year-old cartoon girl who is kind, adventurous, and smart (she's bilingual!). She displays all the qualities you want in your own daughter, like always obeying her parents and never asking her dad for money. She's so friendly that your daughter will likely invite her to her birthday parties for not one but several years, demanding Dora plates, cups, balloons, napkins, wrapping paper, cakes, ponies wearing Dora clothes, etc. If there's something that needs to be purchased for the party, it will have Dora's face on it. If it doesn't, the birthday is ruined.

To better equip you for your future, let me explain every Dora episode ever made (which is easy because every episode is the same). Dora and her best friend, an overly friendly monkey named Boots (whom Dora's parents let roam freely around their house without a leash), are tasked with a mission, such as return a book to the library or rescue someone from a hot-air balloon or travel to space (all of which sound like completely reasonable things to ask of a seven-year-old girl, right?).

Once the mission is in place, Dora and Boots call on their friend, "Map," to show them the path to their journey. Map sings a song that's so annoyingly catchy you will begin to sing it in the shower, in the car, and in important work meetings with your boss.[2] During the journey, Dora and Boots will face two obstacles. Sometimes it's a troll bridge. Sometimes it's a forest of talking trees. Sometimes it's a large lake that conveniently has a rowboat, oars, and two life jackets (just their sizes) next to it (talk about a stroke of good fortune!).

Should the animator forget to place the life jackets by the lake, there's no need to worry: Dora also wears a backpack that talks, sings, and contains exactly the right tools she needs to complete her mission. Is it raining? Backpack will have rainboots in it. Is Boots stuck in the icky, sticky sand? Backpack has a rope to help pull him out. In the mood to time travel? Tough. This is impossible, even for Backpack.

(NOTE: Could you imagine if they made a backpack like this for dads? Wherever you are, whatever you are doing, all you have to do is reach in a bag and you'll have exactly what you need—like a homing device that can locate your lost remote control or a picture of Brad Pitt when you're trying to get your wife in the mood? If you're an inventor and think you can create something like this, call me. We'll market it and go halvsies.)

Another problem Dora and Boots typically encounter is Swiper the Fox, who is always trying to steal their shit. Most of the time, Dora and Boots (and your daughter, if she's old enough to talk) can stop him, with a stern, raised hand in the "stop" position and three forceful rounds of the phrase, "Swiper, no swiping!" That's it. No, I'm not joking. This phrase magically deters the cunning young fox from swiping anything, much like your cut-off shorts magically deterred your high school sweetheart from making out

---

[2] If he doesn't have a daughter, watch out: He'll fire you. If he does have a daughter, watch out: He'll harmonize.

with you in public. Could you imagine if this tactic worked in other walks of life?

- "Hey, hey! Burglar, no burglaring!"
- "White guy, no dancing!"
- "Wife, no spending!"

It'd be nice if everyone responded to this phrase by stopping, but I have a feeling that wouldn't happen. Best-case scenario they'd laugh at you. Most likely scenario, they'd taser you in the face.

Occasionally, though, Swiper succeeds in stealing the item (or items), but instead of running off with the loot, he just hides it in the woods in the most obvious places. Seriously, he does such a poor job at hiding the items that it'd take longer for you to yawn than it would to find everything for Dora. He's like a classroom bully who won't leave you alone, takes your lunch money, and then "hides" it in your bedroom . . . on your bed . . . in plain sight.

If Swiper is teaching our daughters not to steal, great! But if the lesson here is on how to stop a bad guy, I'm worried that our daughters are in for a rude awakening—and a great deal of trouble. Better sign her up for taekwondo immediately, just in case the stern, raised hand in the "stop" position and repetitive dialogue doesn't work.

Once Dora and Boots get by Swiper and overcome their two obstacles, they arrive at their final destination and complete their mission. Everyone is happy and celebrates. This is made official once they sing the "WE DID IT!" song, another fun tune that sears itself permanently into your subconscious. It's a mix of English and Spanish words that, when translated exclusively to English, goes something like this:

We did it! We did it! Yeah!
I know you can't believe it but your daughter really loves this show (It's true! It's true! It's true!)

And in a minute we'll hit you with commercials so you have to buy her
Dora shoes (Oh yeah! That's right! Suck it!)
We did it! We did it! Yeah!

When the episode mercifully ends, you can kick up your feet, relax, and turn back on ESPN, right? Wrong-o! Once your daughter exhausts herself from watching those twenty-two-minute episodes of her favorite little explorer, she'll ask you to *read* a Dora book to her. I've got bad news for you, pal: The plots of the books are identical to the TV shows. It's as if the writing team ran out of ideas and decided that the only way to make more money (and additionally torture dads in the process) was to rehash the same story. It sucks your will to live. Really, you can't believe that you have to relive the same painful show you just watched. Worse yet, when reading the book, you have to attempt to perform the voices. On the bright side, you can turn to your dad friends who also have daughters and say smart and prophetic things like, "I thought the book about Dora becoming a Snow Princess was *way* better than the TV episode. They really botched it by cutting the third Backpack scene. But hey, the show is never as good as the book, am I right?"

I know what you're thinking, *Why do I care about all of this?* Here's why: If you don't mentally prepare to watch the same show over and over and over and over and over and over and over and over and over again, your brain will explode. It will. Trust me. And your wife won't appreciate this for many reasons, most notably because it's tough to remove brain-splatter stains from couch cushions.

WHY LITTLE GIRLS LOVE DORA

Dora the Explorer symbolizes everything a little girl wants to be. She's brave, has lots of friends, and, most important, is on television. She wears shorts year-round, except for when she's called on to be a princess—and then she's draped in the most beautiful of gowns. Her parents allow her to roam freely around the world (and universe) and rarely call her cell phone to check up on her (while I've never seen her with a cell phone, it's pretty clear that there has to be one in her backpack). Her friends are wild, exotic animals like an iguana and a big red chicken—and they all talk! Plus, after watching every episode about 450 times, I can confirm it: Dora the Explorer has never once been asked to eat a vegetable in her life.

You can try to hide Dora's existence from your daughter all you want, but she'll find out about her. Whether it's because your sitter lets her watch an episode or her grandma buys her a Dora toothbrush, somehow, some way she'll meet Dora. And once that happens, it's all over.

I once read about a dad in Table Rock, Nebraska, who sold his television and threatened to turn everyone in the town into "mud-sliders," whatever that is, if they so much as mentioned Dora in front of his little girl. The town stayed silent and this dad's house was Dora-free for two months (a Guinness world record!), but then his daughter saw a magazine on a newsstand that had Dora on the cover. Immediately she knew they were destined for friend-ship. Moments later, her dad turned the vendor into a mudslider. He's now serving thirty-to-life.

Dora has been a staple in my house for several years now. No matter how hard I try to escape her adventures, I can't. Just as one daughter starts to show signs of outgrowing her, the next daughter falls in love with her and the process repeats itself all over again. I keep hoping someone starts a rumor that Dora grew up to be a wicked witch and, after dark, turns into a fire-breathing dragon who lurks in the closets of little kids and eats them in their sleep. Unfortunately, that has yet to happen and my daughters still view her as the lovable little girl who takes them on adventures and teaches them Spanish.

I guess it could be worse. She could be teaching them French.

Dad Lesson

If you don't have a DVR, get one and record every episode of Dora you can find. This will come in handy when you need to distract your daughter, like when she keeps putting her greasy hands all over your baseball-card collection or when she asks you about sex. Just sit her down, press "play," and you have it made. Also, to make sure you don't miss your favorite shows, like reruns of *Walker Texas Ranger* and *Desperate Housewives*, install a second TV in your garage and hope your wife doesn't find out (that you watch *Desperate Housewives*, not that you have the spare TV).

SURVIVING DORA

When all is said and done, the best way to survive the "Dora Years" is to fully embrace it. My wife thinks I'm crazy—a claim that FactCheck.org rates as "Mostly True." But the real truth is that once you accept certain facts in your life—you can't hit a 90-mph fastball, Sweetest Day is real, you aren't more attractive than Justin Timberlake (you're equally attractive), etc.—you can enjoy things a little more. Case in point:

Dora used to drive me insane. The sound of her voice evoked nails scraping along a chalkboard, assuming that the chalkboard also screamed at you and poked you in the eyes. There isn't a day in my house where Dora doesn't rear her football-shaped head in some way, be it television, computer, sippy cup, or fruit snacks (yes, she even bullies her way into your food).

Instead of fighting it, I decided to make Dora my new BFF, too. Now I jump at the opportunity to watch it with my girls, using that time to snuggle on the couch with them (and sneak in a quick nap). I placed a picture of her on my office wall, next to my daughters, to remind me that life's too short to get overly annoyed by a cartoon and, if you can't beat 'em, join 'em. This has had the unintentional side benefit of freaking out my boss, who now thinks I'm a little "off" and has stopped inviting me to meetings (Score!). And, when my wife suggests watching something awful on TV, like anything-other-than-baseball/basketball/football/hockey/curling/*Desperate Housewives*, I turn to the kiddos and say, "Who wants to watch Dora?" She's saved me from a lot of low-grade reality-show watching and for that I am forever grateful.

The Dora Drinking Game

For some of you, acceptance of Dora may be difficult. After all, not everyone who hates broccoli can force themselves to acquire the taste. But this book is all about helping you survive having a daughter, and learning to love Dora is an essential survival tactic that you can't ignore. So to ease you in, I've developed a Dora drinking game. It works as follows:

1. Grab a Dora DVD from your local library or cue up your DVR'd episodes.
2. Send your wife and your daughter (if she's already been born) off to your in-laws' house for the evening.
3. Grab a case of your favorite beer.[3]
4. Close all the blinds and lock the doors. (Trust me, you don't want any witnesses.)
5. Remove all breakable objects.
6. Press "Play all."

Once the first episode starts, take a drink every time:

- An animal talks
- Counting is required

---

[3] I recommend avoiding shots of hard liquor if you want to survive the night.

- Map repeats the path to complete your mission
- Dora talks in Spanish
- Dora asks you to repeat what she says
- Dora asks you to "Say it louder"
- The Grumpy Old Troll appears (ignore his nudity and focus on his impressive beard)
- Dora sings "Come on! ¡*Vamanos!*"
- Dora says "Swiper, no swiping!"
- Swiper swipes something
- A mission is accomplished
- Dora says, "I couldn't have done it without you."
- Dora and Boots stare at the screen awkwardly and blink while waiting for you to tell them your favorite part of the day.

If you don't drink alcohol, don't worry: Once Dora enters your life you will! At worst you can always do this game with water but it's a lot less fun. It also increases your likelihood of having to pee in the middle of the night. Thankfully, with beer, you're much more likely to ralph all over your living room floor, saving you the nighttime trips to the bathroom. The ralphing has little to do with the alcohol and more to do with watching four straight hours of Dora.[4] But this is part of the cleansing process. Once it's out of your system, you'll be able to watch the show for hours and hours on end. You may even find yourself singing along with the songs and bonding with your daughter on which Dora character is your favorite (the correct answer is Dora).

I can't promise that you'll ever completely love Dora, but I can promise you that if you learn to tolerate her, you'll quickly become your daughter's BFF, too. It's a pretty great feeling

---

[4]These four hours will feel like an eternity, much like clothes shopping at the mall with your wife or your high school geometry class. Stay strong—it will eventually come to an end, I promise.

coming downstairs on a Saturday morning, curling up with (pink) sippy cups of milk, and watching your daughter smile each time Dora comes on the screen. Just make sure you aren't still following the Dora drinking game rules. Otherwise it could get messy.

Chapter 6

Learn to Like Tea

(AND OTHER BABY DOLL–RELATED
ACTIVITIES)

One of the many gifts your daughter will receive in her early years will be a tea set. They range from pink sets to princess sets to silver monogrammed sets that are actually more valuable than your fine china.[1] No matter how fancy the set is, it will still serve the same flavors of fake tea that all girls' tea sets serve. These flavors include:

- Tea
- Double Tea
- Double Bubble Tea
- Cold Tea
- Hot Tea
- Strawberry Tea
- Chocolate Tea
- Smoothie Tea
- Coffee Tea
- Flower Water Tea (This is my daughters' favorite kind to serve)
- Lemonade (For when she runs out of tea)

Tea parties are rarely planned and happen spur of the moment, like just after lunch or in the morning when you're running late for work. They can take as little as a few minutes or last as long as February. Any room in the house can host a party, though your wife prefers you keep it in the dining room, so as to not get fake crumbs on the ottoman.

After having sat through my fair share of tea parties, I have learned something very valuable. I don't care how macho you are: When your daughter hands you a cup of make-believe tea, you drink it. End of story.

---

[1]"Fine china" are those expensive plates your wife insisted you put on your wedding registry instead of an Xbox. They are also known as "the plates you've never used."

WHAT'S IN A TEA SET?

When her first tea set arrives, it could include a variety of things. Our set includes one teapot, one sugar bowl, one vase (and a plastic flower to go in it—hence the Flower Water Tea), four place settings, and two cookies. Apparently the makers of the tea set didn't want to include four cookies because they thought it would be funny to start fights.

"I want a cookie!" says your daughter.

"I want a cookie too!" says her friend.

"Me too!!" says the stuffed bunny rabbit who, until the moment, had never voiced an opinion about anything.

"Can't all of you share the cookies?" says a sensible and handsome dad (you).

"How can we share the cookies, dad? They aren't real! Now drink your Coffee Tea before you head to work as a fire-fighting polar-bear trainer."

Unless you had several older sisters who enjoyed torturing you, or a lonely great aunt who stopped by every Sunday for a little great-aunt/great-nephew "bonding time," you probably never have had the opportunity to be part of a tea party. For all you know, a tea party is something only little girls do. But that's 100 percent false. A tea party is also something dads who have little girls do, too.

That's why it's important for you to learn all there is to know about tea parties, including who to expect on the guest list and the Ten Commandments of Properly Participating in a Tea Party.

Let me walk you through what the coming years hold for you. At times you may need to look away—perhaps because this information is too graphic for you, perhaps because you spotted some really cool *SportsCenter* highlight out of the corner of your eye. Either way, proceed with caution. Your life may depend on it. But probably not.

THE GUEST LIST

Once your daughter discovers tea parties, she makes *you* a permanent member of her guest list. There is a good reason for this: You always seem to be sitting, making you very accessible to *taking part* and not very accessible to *escaping*. Your wife occasionally gets a seat at the tea party table, but most of the time she gets out of it by smartly pretending to be too busy "doing laundry" or "making dinner" or "buying you new clothes so you'll stop wearing that Nirvana T-shirt you've been rocking since high school." And your daughter buys these excuses, no matter how fabricated they are and how hard they are to believe (I mean, come on, you still *totally* rock that Nirvana T-shirt).

Once it's been decided that you are in (and you are *always* in), the next step is picking the rest of the participants. I find that selecting the guest list is one of the most interesting parts of the process. Your daughter is the main member of the selection committee and chooses at her will.

Making Small Talk

The guest list ranges from friends (who don't have to be present to actually attend the party) to other family members (who also don't have to be present to attend) to dolls and stuffed animals to imaginary friends—at least, you think that they are imaginary. I guess it's entirely possible that your daughter could have real friends with ridiculous names like "Schmerna," "Pinky Linky Maninky," and "Sue."

You get to meet these characters one by one, often having to carry on fake conversations with them. This sounds miserable, but, in fact, it's one of the more entertaining parts of the tea party.

"So, Schmerna, how'd you get a name like that?"

"Your parents were both circus performers *and* had encounters with aliens? You don't say."

"And you have a twin brother named 'Cablerna'?"

"And you can teleport through time?"

And so on. I found this to be a great way to practice your improv skills. I also found it to be an excellent way to make passive-aggressive comments toward your wife if she, by chance, happens to be standing somewhere within earshot.

"So you're married? How long?"

"Eight years! That's crazy. And how often do you nag your husband?"

"You don't nag at all?! I can't believe it. Even when he forgets some menial little task like taking out the garbage for collection on time or wishing you a happy anniversary? That's so amazing of you. I can't believe you cut him slack because he's been working long days and he's tired when he gets home."

"Wow. I'm sure he doesn't *expect* foot rubs every night, but I'm sure he really appreciates them."

At this point, your daughter might have begun listening to your conversation and note something like, "Dad, stop talking to Schmerna about silly things like foot rubs. Also, why is mom putting your pillow on the couch?"

Make-believe guests come with inherent advantages, such as never making a mess, never overstaying their welcome, and never pointing out that your grass needs cutting. It's why imaginary friends are often preferable to real guests, like, say, your mother-in-law. They are kind and well-mannered and will give you a piece of their make-believe dessert every time you ask for it.

Connecting with Stuffed Animals

Sometimes, imaginary friends and nonpresent family members are replaced by baby dolls and stuffed animals. This is the perfect opportunity to try and sneak your Pete Rose bobblehead into the mix.[2] Nine out of ten times, your daughter won't allow it,[3] citing that he's a boy and not allowed to attend a tea party (NOTE: This rule and regulation doesn't apply to you for some reason. When asked why, the response most typically given is, "You're not a boy, you're a daddy!")

Unless you're up for giving her that biology lesson and are prepared to handle an onslaught of questions, I find it's best to just accept this response and move on.

Dad Lesson

Never, under any circumstances, try to put real tea in the tea cups. This is important for many reasons—if you do it once, you'll have to do it all the time, real spills are worse to clean up than fake spills, and once those cups are sticky, they are sticky forever. Besides, real tea sucks.

THE TEN COMMANDMENTS OF PROPERLY PARTICIPATING IN A TEA PARTY

While the ebb and flow of tea parties changes a bit based on a number of factors (who's invited, how many princess dresses are clean, whether or not your daughter took her afternoon nap), there are a certain set of rules, or commandments, if you will, that you have to abide by in order to have a successful tea party. These commandments were presented years ago, by a prophetic woman named Mosesia, who led the exodus of the Israelites out of Egypt, parted the Red Sea, and came to this wicked cool place called

---

[2]I mean come on, the poor guy has been boxed up in the garage for a couple of years now. If that doesn't warrant a few cups of delicious fake tea, I don't know what does!

[3]Much like how those heartless bastards running Major League Baseball won't allow Mr. Charlie Hustle his rightful spot at baseball's biggest tea party of them all, the Hall of Fame.

Mount Sinai. It was here where she received the Ten Commandments of Properly Participating in a Tea Party from the most holiest of all, Martha Stewart. She carved them into two rocks, presented them to her followers and then sold them at all major retailers for $19.95 (plus tax). Thankfully I was able to get a copy of them for half price.

Without further ado, here are the Ten Commandments of Properly Participating in a Tea Party:

1. **Commandment 1:** When your daughter says the tea party has started, you drop everything—the remote, chores, the copy of *Cosmo* that featured that compatibility quiz your wife insisted you fill out—and sit down for some tea.

2. **Commandment 2:** Make sure your place setting includes all the necessary pieces, including tea cup, saucer, and spoon. NOTE: If you can't find the spoon that matches your set (and you almost never will), it is acceptable to substitute a spoon from your utensil drawer, so long as you also bring back a cookie for your hostess.

3. **Commandment 3:** Drink every last drop of tea served to you. Doesn't matter if that's three cups or 1,100 cups. You are there with one job and one job only, and that's to drink copious amounts of fake tea. Just do it.

4. **Commandment 4:** The number of scoops of sugar you want in your tea is determined by the number of scoops your daughter wants to give you. Taste and health concerns matter not.

5. **Commandment 5:** No matter how many times the teapot is spilled, it will still contain plenty of tea.

6. **Commandment 6:** Always engage your fellow guests, whether they be real, stuffed, or make believe.

7. **Commandment 7:** Never question your hostess about her food menu and be willing to try whatever she serves, even if it is ice cream broccoli stew.

8. **Commandment 8:** Always wear a shirt, preferably one that doesn't smell like yesterday.[4]

9. **Commandment 9:** Every once in a while, let your hostesses stay up a bit past her bedtime to pour you a few more cups. They will be the best cups you've ever tasted.

10. **Commandment 10:** Always compliment your hostess on every cup of tea she pours you. This is perhaps the most important rule on the list. It is also the one that will produce the most smiles, on both her face and yours.

If you abide by all of these commandments, you'll be sure to provide your daughter with memories of tea parties that will last her a lifetime. Unfortunately, a lifetime in kid years is only about six hours, so you'll likely be having a minimum of four tea parties a day. This is also the number two reason dads try to force their daughters into playing sports. The number one reason is ballet.

Dad Lesson

Did you know that the Ten Commandments of Properly Participating in a Tea Party aren't the only set of commandments dads who have daughters must live by? There's also the Ten Commandments of Buying Her Birthday Presents, the Ten Commandments of Teaching Her to Love Sports, and the Ten Commandments of How to Get Her to Take a Dive for You When You Forgot Something Super Important to Your Wife.

---

[4]Sounds like a perfect opportunity to break out that Nirvana T-shirt!

Chapter 7

Extra Innings: When Bedtimes Go Awry

(AND YOU THOUGHT GETTING YOUR WIFE INTO BED WAS DIFFICULT)

A h, bedtime. A few moments of quiet, restful, winding-down bonding between fathers and daughters. *Goodnight Moon*, a lullaby, a peck on the forehead, and it's lights out. Right?

Well, sorta. It can also be a loud, chaotic, drawn-out process that leaves everyone exhausted, frustrated, and ... confusingly, awake.

BEDTIME ROUTINES

Bedtime generally comes with *bedtime rituals*, and I'm a firm believer in bedtime rituals, even for myself (just ask my wife). For years I've abided by a seven-step process that goes something like this:

Step 1: Change into old Ohio University shorts from college (you know, the one with holes in them).
Step 2: Hop into bed.
Step 3: Wink at wife.
Step 4: Watch as wife ignores wink.
Step 5: Kiss wife on cheek to let her know I'm serious.
Step 6: Watch as wife puts on second pair of sweatpants over the pair she's already wearing to let me know *she's* serious.
Step 7: Turn on *SportsCenter* and drift off to sleep the moment they say something about hockey.

Getting your daughter into a bedtime ritual is a little trickier. You'd think it'd be as simple as this: brush teeth, give hugs, confirm that there are no monsters in her closet, turn on nightlight, leave as she falls asleep. But it's not. This process involves an elaborate routine of hygiene maintenance, books, songs, and stalling that can take anywhere from thirty minutes to eleven hours. It's also a routine that involves not two, but three people: you, your daughter, and her baby doll. This will test your fatherly skills. It will also prove that your daughter, much like her mother, is already smarter than you.

BEDTIMES AND BABY DOLLS

Your daughter's baby doll is not just another nighttime friend, she's part of your family. Your daughter becomes very close to her. Heck, *you* have become close to her—after all, she's not only involved in the bedtime routine, but in most other things as well, including tea parties, fashion shows, car rides, and plopping parties (I'd rather not get too deep into this one, just know that during a plopping party there are two plops in every toilet: first hers, which causes you to cheer loudly, then her baby doll's head, which causes you to cheer not so loudly). Her baby doll is so important that she's an integral part of bedtime. The sooner you accept this, the better.

When my eldest daughter turned two and we moved her from a crib in to a big-girl bed (a twin bed), we started a new routine. We said goodnight to mom, gave her kisses, and headed up the long flight of stairs to our upstairs bathroom. We'd brush our teeth, making sure we got every last tooth. *Top. Bottom. Back side. Other back side. Tongue. Spit. Wipe spit that missed sink and landed on floor. Dry face on hand towel. March into bed.*[1] We'd read a book and then I'd sing a song of her choice, which generally boiled down to either *The Itsy Bitsy Spider* or the theme song from *Charles in Charge* (a list of acceptable bedtime songs is discussed later in this chapter). I'd then give her a kiss, tuck her in, say "goodnight," and leave the room.

---

[1] We don't actually march. A more realistic description includes me nagging her, prodding her, carrying her, and eventually dropping her into her bed. If I'm lucky she won't get up as I'm turning on the nightlight so we have to repeat the process all over again.

About a week into the routine, my daughter brought her baby into the bathroom with us (which, at this point, had been banned due to the aforementioned plopping parties).

"Hey, you can't bring her in here, sweetie. She has to stay outside of the bathroom."

"But, dad, she has to brush her teeth too."

"She does?"

"Of course she does."

"But her mouth doesn't even open . . . ?"

"That just means I'll have to brush them extra hard."

I assumed this was a one-time thing, but even if it wasn't, so what? Who was I to deny Baby Number One[2] from practicing proper dental hygiene? After all, it's number three on the list of most important skills you can teach a child, falling just behind dialing 911 in an emergency situation and throwing a backdoor slider. Also, I've seen what my daughter feeds Baby Number One—milk, juice, French fries, plastic veggies, sneakers, the remote control, whatever she can find in the couch cushions, fridge magnets, and garbage. Baby Number One shouldn't have to suffer through baby doll bad breath. Neither should my daughter, who kisses her all the time.[3]

So all three of us brushed our teeth. *Top. Bottom. Back side. Other back side. Tongue. Spit. Wipe spit that missed sink and landed on floor. Dry face on hand towel. March into bed.* I didn't have a toothbrush for Baby Number One, so I used my wife's. To this day my wife doesn't know that.[4]

---

[2]Yes, Baby Number One was her official name—I'm not quite sure why she named her that, but from what I've gathered from talking with friends this is fairly common and there's a 70 percent chance you're daughter's doll will be named Baby Number One too. The other 30 percent name their dolls Princess Fallullah Von Pretty Girl, Toots, or Megan.

[3]Then again, maybe she deserves it for feeding her baby doll garbage.

[4]Wait, if she reads this book she will find out about it. Crap. I hope either the editor cuts this part or, when she reads this part, she gets distracted by my rugged good looks and forgets all about it. At the very least, I hope that by the time this book is published, we've purchased a more husband-friendly couch that doesn't promote scoliosis.

Once in bed, I picked out a book to read to my daughter. My mind is a little foggy on this detail, but I can say with some confidence we read *The Little Engine That Could*, *The Cat in the Hat*, or *The Bill James Historical Baseball Abstract*. I finished up the book and went to kiss my daughter goodnight when she said, "What about Baby Number One?"

"What about Baby Number One?"

"Doesn't she get a book too?"

This didn't seem unreasonable, so I agreed. It seemed a lot more unreasonable when Baby Number One picked the longest book on our bookshelf. But I read it anyway because, quite frankly, I'm a sucker.

After the book ended, I let my daughter pick a song. I sang it. As I started to stand up, she chimed in again.

"Doesn't Baby Number One get a song too?"

"No, sweetie, Baby Number One doesn't get a song too."

"But how is she supposed to fall asleep without a song?"

This was a good question. After all, how *was* Baby Number One supposed to fall asleep without a song? Also, how was Baby Number One supposed to fall asleep considering her eyes were painted on her face and don't close? I could be wrong, but I think it's safe to assume that this is the number-one cause of baby doll insomnia. It's also why baby dolls are creepy.

"Okay, I guess she can have a song too. What does she want?"

"How about *Charles in Charge*?"

So I belted it out like a Broadway singer, hitting note after note, using inflection where it was needed, and adding in some dance steps just to give it an extra level of pizzazz. It may have been my best rendition of that catchy TV show theme to date. Unbelievably, Baby Number One seemed unimpressed.

Finally, I gave my daughter a kiss and tucked her in. I could see where this was heading, so without instruction I also gave Baby Number One a kiss on the forehead and tucked her in tightly.

"Dad, don't kiss her on the forehead. Kiss her on the lips."

"On the lips?"

"Don't worry, she brushed her teeth."

And that, my friends, is how my two-year-old daughter got me to make out with a baby doll.

BILLBOARD'S TOP 20 BEDTIME SONGS THAT DADS SING TO DAUGHTERS

One of the upsides of having a daughter is that you have a lengthy list of bedtime songs to choose from when selecting a late-night lullaby. If you had a son, your only acceptable options would be Cat Stevens's "Father & Son" and Dan Fogelberg's "Leader of the Band." (Yeah, I know, that still would have been pretty awesome.) Thankfully, Billboard has been tracking the popularity of songs that dads sing to daughters for the past thirty years. I've provided you with the top twenty. Instead of listing them in order, though, I decided to break them into three subcategories so they are easier for you to remember. They are as follows:

The Usual List
1. Twinkle, Twinkle, Little Star
2. The Itsy Bitsy Spider
3. London Bridge Is Falling Down
4. Oh My Darling Clementine
5. Mary Had a Little Lamb
6. She'll Be Comin' Round the Mountain
7. Rock a Bye Baby
8. When You Wish Upon a Star
9. Row, Row, Row Your Boat

The Theme Song List

1. Charles in Charge
2. Where Everybody Knows Your Name (*Cheers*)
3. (Theme from) *The Monkees*
4. As Long as We've Got Each Other (*Growing Pains*)
5. Nothing's Gonna Stop Me Now (*Perfect Strangers*)
6. More Than Meets the Eye (*Transformers*)[5]

The Miscellaneous List

1. Take Me Out to the Ballgame (classic song that will connect her with sports)
2. Take Me Out to the Ballgame, Hometown Team Edition (instead of "Root, root, root, for the *home team*," insert the name of your hometown team. Unless your hometown team is the Cubs. Then stick with *home team*.)
3. Don't Know Much (Aaron Neville's voice is proof that there is a heaven)
4. I Need a Hero (by Bonnie Tyler, though change the main lyrics to "Dad Is My Hero." Also, feel free to ad lib where applicable.)
5. Anything by Metallica

Commit these songs to memory and I promise that your daughter will not only feel a stronger connection to you, she will also request that, from now on, her mother takes her to bed.

WHEN BEDTIME GOES INTO EXTRA INNINGS

Not all daughters sleep with a baby doll. Take my middle daughter, for example. She didn't care if her doll (named Toots—pronounced like it rhymes with "foots") brushed her teeth, nor did

---

[5]Be sure to make laser noises when singing.

she want to share a bed with her.[6] But she still found a way to stall, and, if your daughter is like her, bedtime will be like a very intense game of baseball that plays out like this:

Every night is the bottom of the ninth. There are two outs and you have a one-run lead. You are doing your best to close this game out, while she stands at the plate, doing her best to send it to extras. You stand at the edge of her bed and throw pitch after pitch of "goodnights" and "see you in the mornings," which she fouls off with swings of "Just one more story, please" and "I need to pee again." These grueling at-bats last for several minutes until finally, after the stadium (night)light comes on, you drop the hammer.

"That's it! It's late. No more talking. Go to sleep. Good. Night." Close door. Game over. Pump fist. Point to the sky. Get congratulated by wife with a sportsmanlike "good game" pat-on-the-butt.

But it's not over. In fact, it's only beginning. Just as you start to head down the stairs, you hear a soft voice come from her bedroom:

"Dad, we forgot to say prayers."

HOME RUN! GAME TIED!

Dads can deny a daughter a lot of things—ice cream for breakfast, getting her ears pieced, a Twitter account, dating, those awful socks with the separate toes sewn into them—but we can't deny her prayers. Heck, I remember being a young kid, sitting with my mom on the edge of my bed, praying for my family, my friends, and my Cincinnati Reds to win the pennant. It is a tradition that has carried on since the invention of bedtime rituals, so why can't it be a part of the ritual now?

I'll tell you why. Because your sweet, adorable, loving daughter will, like mine, pray for everything under the sun—and everything

---

[6]She claims Toots hogs the pillows—though, after checking on both in the middle of the night, it's clear to me that Toots is merely trying not to fall off the bed and is hanging on to the pillow for dear life.

above the sun, behind the sun, inside the sun, related to the sun, not related to the sun, divorced from the sun, and birthed by the sun. And that's before you move on to the moon. If she's met a person, she'll pray for him. She also will pray for that person's parents, whether she's met them or not. And, occasionally, she will try to sneak in a quick prayer for her Cabbage Patch doll, Sylvia, who, in all honesty, needs it considering the way she gets hurled around your house.

By the time she moves on to inanimate objects, it's an hour past her bedtime. It's an hour past *your* bedtime. Your wife will finally come in like a pitching coach who has seen enough and relieve you of your duties. "Not your day today, is it, Ace?" she'll say. And with a pitiful "nice try" pat-of-the-butt, she'll send you to the showers.

The best you can do is rest up for tomorrow. It'll probably be another long night.

Dad Lesson

When your daughter has a nightmare there are only three acceptable ways to dealing with it. 1) Let her sleep in your bed. 2) Sleep in her bed with her. 3) Tell her about the time you chose Carson Palmer over Peyton Manning in your fantasy football league and explain why you made that decision. This will not only cause her to forget about her nightmare, it will also make her refuse to ever have another nightmare just so she doesn't have to hear that story again.

HOW TO GET HER TO SLEEP

After you've exhausted all your bedtime rituals and she's run out of stalls, it's time to finally get her to sleep. This is no easy task. But if Rudy could overcome his physical shortcomings to make the Notre Dame Fighting Irish football team, you can certainly overcome your lack-of-getting-her-to-go-to-sleep abilities. I don't expect you to conquer this overnight, but with a little help from a tired, more experienced dad (me), I do believe you can successfully get your daughter to sleep and still have plenty of time to be shot down by your wife for sex.[7] Here's the five-step process to getting your daughter to (finally) fall asleep.

Step 1. Compliment her PJ selection.

By telling her how much you like her pajamas, you're letting her know that she's had some control on the night and that she's able to make the smart decision to get some rest.

Step 2. Let her know that if it were up to you, she wouldn't have a bedtime.

Daughters are more likely to fall asleep if they trust you. By letting her know how absurd you think this "bedtime rule" is (and making it clear that it has been imposed by her mother), you'll get her to let down her guard and feel like you are on her side.

Step 3. Gently brush her hair with your hands.

This calming action will put an end to her bouncing around and "trying to find a comfortable position." It will also give you an opportunity to use your other hand to get sports scores from your smartphone.

Step 4. Persuade her to try "resting her eyes."

Tell her she doesn't have to sleep, just lay there with her eyes closed. You can attempt to show her by example but be forewarned: You wife will not wake you up and move you off your daughter's nightstand.

---

[7]This shouldn't take longer than half a second.

Step 5: Pretend that you have to go to the bathroom and say that you'll be right back when you are finished.

It's the only legitimate excuse you can use to exit the room that:

1. Your daughter understands;
2. Has a variable timetable so your daughter can't be sure when you will officially return. By the time you check in on her several minutes later, she'll be fast asleep.

And if she's not asleep, beware: It's possible your daughter is a zombie.

THE BEST PART ABOUT BEDTIMES

Whether it's preventing her baby doll from getting gingivitis, praying for the neighborhood possum that she befriended several weeks ago, or any other regular bedtime ritual that happens in your house, know that eventually you are going to miss this. A lot. You are going to miss those extra few moments you get with your daughter, doing whatever silly thing it is that she wants to do that leads up to the best part of the night, which is giving her a hug and kiss, tucking her in, and hearing her say those four words that will melt your heart forever:

"I love you, daddy."

This part of the bedtime ritual will get you through any night, even ones when your wife is wearing two pairs of sweatpants.

HALFTIME QUIZ

Now that you've finished the first half of this book, I want to make sure you've retained the valuable information I've supplied. Here's a ten-question quiz designed to help you gauge just how far you've come in your soon-to-be or recent challenge of raising a daughter. I'm just as confident you'll ace this as I was that O.J. didn't do it. Also, if you're not good at taking quizzes, don't worry—I'm not good at making up quizzes.

So take your time and think long and hard before making your pick. At the end we'll review, grade, and move on to part two of *Oh Boy, You're Having a Girl,* where I'll not only tell you how to deal with your daughter's first crush, but I'll also reveal who will win the next Super Bowl (*he doesn't know that . . . or does he?* Hmm . . . better read on).

By the way, all the correct answers are D.

What is the appropriate age to let your daughter get her ears pierced?

A. Right after she's born.

B. When she's ten.

C. Is "never" an option?

D. When she is old enough to run for president.

Your wife has scheduled family photos. She has dressed both your daughter and herself in all pink. She has purchased a pink shirt and tie for you to wear as well. You:

A. Refuse to take part in the family photos unless everyone dresses in something more masculine, like football helmets.

B. Set the pink shirt and tie on fire to prove a point. (This back-fires, of course, once you see the ransom your wife paid for them printed on the department store receipt and now realize they are unreturnable.)

C. Ask to be traded.

D. Put on the pink shirt and tie and then smile for the photo (but cry in private).

QUESTION 3

The new *Dora the Explorer* special is airing at the same time as game seven of the World Series, in which your favorite team is playing. You:

A. Pretend your daughter did something wrong and send her to her room.
B. Give your wife $500 to take your daughter on a shopping spree.
C. Tell your daughter that Dora has died (I know this one sounds a bit severe, but when you calmly explain your reasoning to your wife she'll surely understand and support your decision: It's GAME SEVEN!)
D. Impulsively buy a second flat-screen TV to set up on the other side of your living room so you both can watch your programs simultaneously while still cuddling on the same couch.

QUESTION 4

Disney on Ice comes to town. You:

A. Pretend like you didn't know about it, even though every other commercial is an advertisement for it.
B. Tell your daughter that while you'd like to take her, your princess gown is at the dry cleaner's and you can't go because you have nothing to wear.
C. Lie to her and tell her you live in another town.
D. Buy tickets immediately. Who are we kidding? Disney on Ice is awesome.

Your wife has to leave early for a work meeting and asks you to dress your daughter. You ask her how to accomplish this and your wife responds, "Whatever you put her in is fine." What she actually means is:

A. Whatever you put her in is fine.

B. While she's never once dressed her in a baseball jersey, she trusts your judgment and if you think a baseball jersey is an acceptable form of clothing for your little daughter, then she fully supports you.

C. Put her in the same thing she wore yesterday no matter how bad it smells.

D. Do not dress her yourself. Call your mom and ask her for help.

After studying the Ten Commandments of Properly Participating in a Tea Party, you know that the most amount of fake tea a dad's body can physically consume is:

A. Ten cups of fake tea.

B. Twenty cups of fake tea.

C. Fifty cups of fake tea.

D. However many cups your daughter says you will drink. (NOTE: It's not so much the ridiculous amount of fake tea that she forces you to drink that will bother you, as it is the number of times you will have to wake up in the middle of the night to fake pee.)

One of your friends is giving you a hard time about having a daughter so you challenge him to a Grill Off! In the middle of the competition, you severely burn your hand. Do you:

A. Admit defeat and have a friend rush you to the emergency room.

B. Ask your friend for a "time-out" so you can assess the damage.

C. Pretend your phone is ringing. Say it's your wife and there's an emergency at home you must attend to. (Make sure it's something believable like your house is on fire or she needs you to sex her badly.)

D. Wrap it in bacon and muscle through the pain.

You are playing coed softball and there is a girl blocking the plate. In the past you would have barreled right through her (after all, you don't block the plate!), but now that you have a daughter, you:

A. Politely ask her to move out of your way.

B. Let her tag you out.

C. Try to flap your arms and fly over her, landing safely on home plate.

D. Still barrel through (after all, she *is* blocking the plate).

What do you teach your daughter to do when she sees a Cubs fan?

A. Boo mercilessly.
B. Boo mercilessly.
C. Boo mercilessly.
D. All of the above.

On a scale of one to ten, how good-looking is the author of this book?

A. He's okay. Maybe a six.
B. Sorry, chief, I'm not into judging guys on their looks. That seems a bit superficial to me.
C. For a guy who's given birth to three daughters, he's really found a way to keep it together.
D. He's an eleven.

Chapter 8

Questions You Never Expected Your Daughter to Ask

(AND HOW TO ANSWER THEM)

From the minute my first daughter was born, I began preparing to answer the hard questions every dad who has daughters is eventually forced to answer. You know, the questions that test your ability as a parent. And, if you're like me and have a photographic memory for facts, you'll be able to quench your young one's thirst for knowledge with honest, dignified answers.

Daughter: *Dad, where do babies come from?*
Me: They are dropped off at the hospital by storks flying through the sky. You were dropped off by one named Marvin. True story.

Daughter: *Dad, how does Santa get into a house if it doesn't have a chimney?*
Me: That's easy—he uses a key that parents hide under the door-mat to come through the front door. If the parents forget, he just picks the lock with Rudolph's antlers.

Daughter: *Dad, why do people like* The Real Housewives?
Me: No one knows.

And so on. It's a dad's job to answer these questions earnestly, in a way your daughter can understand and with an answer that will get you into the least amount of trouble when one day she figures out that your honest and dignified answers are also commonly referred to as "lying." Of course, then you must eventually answer the question, "Why were you lying?"—to which the correct answer is, "You're grounded."

THE CURVEBALLS

But no matter how hard you prepare for these age-old questions, eventually your sweet little angel will throw you a curveball. Allow me to demonstrate with an actual conversation that took place in my house between my eldest daughter and me.

Daughter: Dad, where are your boobs?

(Yes, she actually said it. And, like any intelligent, thoughtful dad, I pretended not to hear it and quickly changed the subject to something that will not get me in trouble with my wife.)

Me: So daughter, you're what, three years old now? I was thinking it's about time we got you a pony.
Daughter: Dad, *I said,* where are your boobs?

In every dad's moment of weakness, he does one of two things:

1. Tells the truth
2. Fakes a stroke

Unfortunately my daughter mistook my fake stroke for a sneeze (my high school drama teacher would have been so disappointed in me). So I sucked it up and went with the truth—which led to this, nearly verbatim, conversation:

Me: Well hon, I don't have boobs.
Daughter: Why don't you have boobs?
Me: Because I'm a boy.
Daughter: Boys don't have boobs?
Me: No, boys don't have boobs.
Daughter: But mom has boobs.
Me: She's not a boy, she's a girl.
Daughter: So only girls have boobs?
Me: Yes, only girls have boobs. Can you stop saying boobs?
Daughter: I don't have boobs. Does that mean I'm a boy?

Me: No, you're a girl.

Daughter: Then where are *my* boobs?

Me: You don't have them yet. One day when you get older you will get boobs.

Daughter: When?

Me: When you're older. Much, much older.

Daughter: How will I know when I'm getting boobs?

Me: When I start to carry a baseball bat around the house.

Daughter: Does that mean that when you're older you will finally get boobs, too?

Me: I hope not.

Daughter: Maybe you can ask Santa for some boobs?

Me: That's okay. I've already asked Santa for enough.

Daughter: Well, I can ask him for you.

Me: You don't have to do that.

Daughter: I don't mind. I have room now that I can cross pony off my list.

I wish I could tell you that this would be the only difficult question your daughter will ask you, but it won't be. Daughters are exceptionally smart (I blame their mothers for this). They will dive deep into your soul, hunting around for the questions that will haunt you the most. At no point will they ever take into consideration how uncomfortable it makes you. Instead, they will fire off questions whenever they see fit (at breakfast, on the drive to grandma's house, in front of your drinking buddies, etc.). The only thing that is 100 percent certain is that she will ask you when your wife isn't around to help answer.

Now, I'm not the best at answering the tough questions, but I'm no rookie either. I've been thrown these pitches time after time, practicing my swing, fouling off question after question until I'm able to give an answer that is not only enough to satisfy my daughter's thirst for knowledge, but also doesn't continually cost me a

> ## Dad Lesson
>
> If your daughter asks a lot of questions, take this as a positive sign. Sure, it'll drive you crazy when she's young, but it will pay off in the long run when she's all grown up and comes to you looking for answers to questions like "How old do I need to be to get married?"[1] and "Have you seen my tampons?"[2]

pony. At first I wasn't the best at changing diapers, but now my wife brags to others that I'm "not terrible" at it. I think it's safe to say I'm "not terrible" at answering these questions, either.[3]

To help you out, I've developed a list of the most common questions you never expected your daughter to ask you and have provided examples of the wrong way and the right way to answer each one. The wrong answers will help you understand what your gut is telling you to say, and your gut (as you well know), generally makes the wrong decisions.[4]

Read them. Rehearse them. Commit them to memory. And whatever you do, don't deviate too much from the answer. I've spent years refining these, and even the slightest change in the wording could lead her to do the unthinkable: ask another question.

DADDY, WHY DON'T YOU SIT DOWN TO PEE?

Wrong Answer: Because if I sat down to pee, I'd probably start working on the crossword puzzle. And, you know me, I love a good

---

[1] The correct response is: Ask me again in ten years.

[2] The correct response is: Is that the name of your fantasy football team?

[3] A "Not Terrible" on the Dad of Daughter Report Card is equivalent to a B. If you ever get it in writing, hang that shit on your fridge.

[4] You don't believe your gut is always wrong? Think of it this way: How many times have you looked at your wife as she climbs over your mountain of dirty clothes on the floor and, as she finally made it into bed, builds a pillow wall to separate her side from yours, and thought, "I think she's giving me a sign to go for it!" That's your gut talking. He's an idiot. (But *my* gut says it's still worth the gamble.)

crossword puzzle and would end up sitting there longer than I should. Then, by the time I got up, it'd be bedtime and I wouldn't be able to do fun things with you, like play Princess Yahtzee or let you jump on me while "we" watch sports. So I really do it as a timesaver.

Why It's the Wrong Answer: In an effort to save time (per your explanation), your daughter will start standing up to pee, leaving puddles on the floor that you will have to clean up. Worse yet, this will always happen at a critical moment of the sporting event you are watching. (I am the only person in history who missed Eli Manning throw the game-winning touchdown in Super Bowl XLII to upset the perfect season of the New England Patriots—all because I was mopping up daughter diddle.) Lesson learned: When giving answers, don't give your daughter ideas. Stick with fairly simple answers that she can understand.

Right Answer: It's because they don't make Dora potty seats in my size.

WHAT COLOR BOW ARE YOU GOING TO WEAR IN YOUR HAIR TO WORK TODAY?

Wrong Answer: "What color don't we have? Brown? Well, I would have loved to have worn a brown one today but since we don't have one I obviously will not be able to wear it. Sorry sweetie."

Why It's the Wrong Answer: Your daughter will tell your wife that the only reason you aren't wearing a bow in your hair to work is because you don't have a brown one. Your wife, who loves you with all her heart, will purposely find (and purchase) a brown bow and let your daughter give it to you. Your daughter will be so excited that you will have no choice but to wear it. Worse yet, your wife, who loves you with all her heart, will suggest (right in front of your daughter) that you have a coworker take a picture of you wearing the bow while at work, so they can see how happy you are wearing it. There is no guarantee your daughter will appreciate this, but there is a 100 percent guarantee this picture will show up on the Internet.

Right Answer: "My office has a strict policy that says boys are not allowed to wear bows in their hair to work. I know, I think it's completely unfair too. I hope one day we live in a world that is tolerant enough to allow boys to wear bows in their hair to work. But until that day, I must follow the rules, no matter how unreasonable they are."

WHY DON'T YOU SLEEP WITH A BABY DOLL?

Wrong Answer: "There's no room for baby dolls. I sleep with your mom and she already takes up too much of the bed."

Why It's the Wrong Answer: RED ALERT: This is a HUGE mistake. This answer—which most certainly will make its way back to your wife—could be interpreted as you calling her "fat." You never make any move toward calling her the F-word. Because if you do, it'll be a long, long time before you ever get to do the other F-word again.[5]

Right Answer: "I don't need baby dolls anymore. If I ever need someone to cuddle, I'll just come in and give you a hug. Hugs from you are the best. Besides, mom makes me keep my baby doll in the closet. Something about "he smells like farts.""

WHY DO YOU SLEEP IN THE SAME BED AS MOM?

Wrong Answer: "Because mom is super afraid that the monsters in our closet are going to come out and eat her in the middle of the

---

[5] I'm talking about fantasy sports, you pervert.

night, so I have to sleep next to her and protect her. You wouldn't want mom to get eaten, would you?"

Why It's the Wrong Answer: By suggesting that there are monsters in the house, you have now scared your daughter to death. There is nothing you can say to undo this. Might as well move your pillow into your daughter's bed, because that's where you'll be spending most of your nights from now on.

Right Answer: "If I didn't sleep next to mom, who would wake her up in the middle of the night when you needed her to help you go potty, get a drink of water, or stay up for no reason whatsoever. Mom would probably sleep through all of that if it weren't for me. You. Are. Welcome."

WHY AREN'T THERE ANY GIRLS IN YOUR FANTASY BASEBALL LEAGUE?

Wrong Answer: Well, sweetie, girls don't want to play fantasy sports because it's a man's game.

Why It's the Wrong Answer: You don't want your daughter thinking she can't be just as good (if not better) than a boy, no matter what the challenge is. It's talk like this that will push her into making terrible life decisions, like doing drugs or taking ballet. It's also a lie, as you'd welcome anyone into your league—male or female—so long as they were:

1. Willing to pay the $100 entry fee.
2. Worse than you at fantasy baseball.

Right Answer: "Because you aren't old enough to join. But over the next few years I'm going to spend countless hours teaching you how to be the best fantasy baseball team owner in the world, that way when you turn fourteen you'll be able to join the league and spend as much time studying fascinating stats like Quality Starts, WHIP, Zone Rating, and BABIP (and no, I didn't make any of those up)."

WHAT'S THAT? (POINTS TO YOUR GENITALS AS YOU GET OUT OF THE SHOWER)

Wrong Answer: "OH MY GOD, HOW DID THAT FALL OUT?!"

Why It's the Wrong Answer: Your daughter is a kind, loving, and *helpful* individual. By acting as if your penis fell out of your body she may be inclined to do the thoughtful thing and try to shove it back up for you. You want no part of that.

Right Answer: "That, my dear, is a poisonous part of the male body. All boys have it and it can kill you. Stay as far away from it as you can, and if any boy ever tries to get it too close to you, head-butt him in the face. Hard."

THE OTHER DAY I SAW YOU AND MOM NAKED IN BED. WHAT WERE YOU DOING?

Wrong Answer: Blank stare.

Why It's the Wrong Answer: This is a knee-jerk reaction that will not only prolong this God-awful moment in your life, it'll send the message to your daughter that she's stumbled upon a subject that makes you nervous. And if I've learned anything about kids (this goes for both girls and boys), it's that once they find a topic they know makes you nervous, their brains go into overdrive and start formulating follow-up questions that are worse. *Why were you on top of her? Why did you keep saying, "Oh yeah"? Why did mom have such a disappointed look on her face?* These questions will not only freak you out, but will also lower your self-esteem. Don't let that happen.

Right Answer: "I was checking her for any cancerous moles and she was doing the same for me. I want to check for them all the time but your mom only likes to check every once in a while. It's a safety issue, really."

SO I CAME FROM MOMMY'S BELLY? HOW DID I GET IN THERE?

Wrong Answer: "Well, sweetie, that's a difficult ... that's a hard one to ... hmmm ... there comes a time when a man and a woman ... um ... decide that ... um ... and your mom thought it would be a good idea if we, you know ... um ... and I thought, *Well, we have a spare bedroom* and ... um ... then we watched the movie *Say Anything,* you know, the one where John Cusack holds the boombox over his head in the rain, which is one of your mom's favorites, and ... um ... and then I ... um ... I looked at her belly and ... well ... I yelled SHAZAM! And then you were in there."

Why It's the Wrong Answer: Your daughter doesn't deserve an answer like this. She is smart and innocent and just plain curious. It's a natural part of life that can be explained rationally and with grace. Hell, it's science, for crying out loud! Give her the most honest answer you have to give.

Right Answer: "I have no idea. Ask your mother."[6]

WILL I EVER HAVE A BABY LIKE MOMMY?

Wrong Answer: When you're much older, there will be a time in your life when you meet someone special and fall in love. You will connect on a very deep level emotionally, physically, and mentally

---

[6] I was really, really bad at science.

and, if all goes well, you will get married and have a beautiful celebration. You'll enjoy sharing your life together until one day, when the time is right, you will make a wish and, if you are lucky enough, you will be blessed with a baby of your own. If you're extra lucky, you'll have an amazing daughter just like I have."

Why It's the Wrong Answer: It gives her the impression that dating is okay. It is not okay.

Right Answer: "Over my dead body."

IF ALL ELSE FAILS

I know there are other uncomfortable questions not covered in this section that will ultimately come up. They will make you cringe. If you are really stuck, just remember: You have a car, a license to drive it, and a nearby playground. Swings, slides, and injuries from falling off the monkey bars are a quick and easy way to change the subject.

Wife: "What happened!?!"

Me: "Oh, man, Rosie was asking me about sex. I didn't know what to do."

Wife: "So you broke her arm!?!"

Me: "No, I took her to the park. She broke her arm all on her own."

Wife: "I'm going to kill you, you know."

Me: "But I ... I ... I ..."

Commence faking a stroke. (And do your high school drama teacher proud this time!)

Chapter 9

She's Sick, Drop Everything!

(AND INVEST IN A DVR)

Runny noses are a natural part of life. You can try to insulate your daughter from germs—by not allowing others to touch her or by putting her in a giant bubble—but ultimately she'll still catch a bug every now and again. (Plus, it's super hard to find those bubbles on Craigslist.)

It's your job, as her father, to make sure she gets the proper care she needs—whether it be medical treatment, emotional support, or surrounding her by vomit buckets—and make her as comfortable as possible. It's also your job to freak out. After all, she is your little girl.

THE DIFFERENCE BETWEEN CARING FOR SONS AND DAUGHTERS

As a boy, you were likely raised to be tough: Have the flu? Deal with it. Broke your ankle? Duct tape it. Swelling up because you sniffed a peanut and it triggered a life-threatening allergic reaction? Quit your whining (and wheezing), get back on the school bus.

That's called tough love. It's how my father took care of me and how his father took care of him. I'm confident that if you traveled back in time, you'd find my great-great-great-great-great-great grandfather telling his son to, "Stop writhing around on the ground in pain and get back to tending to the farm animals. Femurs heal. Cows can't feed themselves!"

Having a daughter isn't quite like that. Injuries or illnesses that occur to your sweet little angel are handled with such soft gloves—and terrifying panic—that the tiniest little scratch is treated as a full-blown medical emergency. Ambulances are called. Gauze and medical tape fill the room. You hug your daughter to stop the tears, but it doesn't work—instead she looks you in the eye and says, "Dad, stop crying, I'll be okay."

Most household accidents and illnesses happen so fast, that you don't have time to prepare yourself. So a situation typically unfolds something like this:

You and your daughter are playing nicely in the living room, probably with something safe like a hammer. While running to jump on you, she trips over her own feet and falls—in what appears to be The Guinness Book of World Records's *world record for slowest slow-motion fall in the history of the universe—onto the carpeted floor. She doesn't cry or make any kind of peep. Your job, as you know, is to remain calm, cool, and collected, as to not panic your daughter and to stay in control of the situation.*

You: "Oh my God! Oh my God! Oh my God!"

Your Wife: "What happened?"

You: "Little Rosie fell! SHE FELL! I'm taking her to the ER."

Your Wife: "What did she hit?"

You: "Her knee. Right on the floor."

Your Wife: "Does it look broken?"

You: "It must be! She's not moving it!"

Your Wife: "That's because *you* are holding it."

You: "I can't believe I took my eye off her for one second. I'll never do that again."

You turn back to your daughter.

You: "It'll be okay, sweetie, I promise. You're not going to die. Daddy's here to take care of you."

Your Wife: "Going to die? She just . . ."

You: "I need the medical emergency kit. Where do we keep it? In the linen closet?"

Your Wife: "What do you need that for?"

You: "It has CPR instructions. I want to be prepared if she has a concussion and passes out."

Your Wife: "From bumping her knee?"

You: "I was reading an article last week on BabyCenter.com that says concussion symptoms might not be visible until *well* after the initial incident that caused the trauma."

Your Wife: "All I see on her knee is what I believe a doctor would diagnose as a 'light scratch.'"

You: "I better take off work this week and take care of her. How long does FMLA cover?"

Your Wife: "I'm leaving you."

For the record, that is just a bluff. She won't leave you for taking extra-special care of your daughter when she's hurt. She'll leave you for A.C. Slater and his killer muscle shirt/hammer pants fashion combo. And, quite honestly, it's hard to blame her.

SICKNESS/INJURY SCENARIOS AND HOW TO HANDLE THEM: SONS VS. DAUGHTERS

To help you better gauge your responses to potential ailments that your daughter may face, I've listed the different ways you react to a daughter versus a son. If you recognize many of the responses that I'd give to a son in these scenarios, it's likely because your dad gave them to you. And although you turned out super awesome, the same won't happen for your daughter unless you take my advice and handle each one of these events with the proper response.

- Injury Scenario: Your child is riding a bike and crashes into some bushes.

  What you say to a son: "Get out of those bushes and back on that bike, you wimp!"

  What you say to a daughter: "Don't move! I'm diving in to save you!"

- Injury Scenario: Your child is complaining of a sore throat.
  What you say to a son: "Gargle some saltwater and stop your complaining, or I'll give you something to complain about!"
  What you say to a daughter: "I bought 197 popsicles for you. They should help ease the pain. Also, I canceled all my meetings so I could spend the day massaging your neck."

- Injury Scenario: Your child falls from a tree and breaks an arm.
  What you say to a son: "That better not be your pitching arm!"
  What you say to a daughter: "I will spend all the money in the world to get you the best doctors and repair that arm immediately! And no, I promise I won't be pulling any money from your wedding fund."

- Injury Scenario: Your child develops a case of the chicken pox.
  What you say to a son: "Do you think Kirk Gibson scratched his chicken pox before going out and clobbering that game-winning home run in the '88 World Series? I don't think so. Toughen up!"
  What you say to a daughter: "Here is a back scratcher and a Brillo pad. Go to town!"

- Injury Scenario: Your child is suffering from a life-threatening disease and needs a kidney transplant.
  What you say to a son: One of your kidneys is failing? Well, that's just an opportunity for your other one pick up the slack and show us what he's made of.
  What you say to a daughter: You can have both of mine. And your mom's. And one from that neighbor kid whom we don't really like that much. Get me an hour and I'll get it for you.

A TYPICAL NIGHT WITH A SNIFFLY DAUGHTER

I'll never forget the first time my middle daughter got sick. It taught me, and can now teach you, how to deal with cold and flu season. Mine was six months old when she got her first bout with cold/flu, and the crisp fall air was a clear sign that absolutely no one in our house was going to get any sleep that night. My wife offered to get up with her, but I told her no. This was a job for dad and I was up for the challenge. I also had to pee, so I had to get up anyway.

I picked up my daughter from her crib—she had awoken again, unable to comfortably lie flat because her nose kept getting stuffed up. We slowly made our way down to the living room couch—I knew it'd be a long night and I didn't want to be confined to her bedroom (specifically because there was no TV with *SportsCenter* in her bedroom). I piled everything that I could find that was soft—pillows, blankets, toilet paper—and built the cushiest, most comfortable couch-bed known to man. It is one of my top three architectural achievements, just after assembling a baby swing and them assembling a *second* baby swing because I accidentally stepped on—and broke—the first baby swing.

I laid down on the couch-bed with my sweet little daughter in my arms. I spent several minutes moving and adjusting, trying to find the perfect level of comfort while keeping her in the upright position to allow her sinuses to drain. This proved particularly difficult because

1. She wouldn't lie still.
2. I forgot to completely clear off the couch before building my couch-bed and now had to deal with a remote control that was moonlighting as a rectal thermometer.

By the time I reached an agreeable level of comfort, I was drenched in sweat. I don't know if you've ever had the opportunity to hold a feverish baby on your chest, but if you have, you know that their tiny bodies are hot. Blazing hot. Some scientists have proved, through math and complicated math, that sick, sleeping babies are the number one cause of global warming. Number two is cow farts.

My daughter finally fell asleep, letting off a quiet snore that I could most certainly deal with, and I drifted off too. It's not how I would have drawn up the playbook for the night, but it's an audible I was happy to call and take. However, the peace lasted for maybe fifteen seconds before she moved her head and buried it into my neck, cutting off 70 percent of the windpipe I use to breathe and forcing my head into a horizontal position that looks about as natural as Barry Bonds did when he had done more than just eat his Wheaties.[1] I desperately needed to move, but I didn't out of fear she would wake up. This is called "Sucking It Up for the Good of the Team" and dads do this all the time.

I finally found a way to fall back to sleep in spite of the pain, but that didn't last long either. Every six minutes or so, my baby daughter would let out back-to-back-to-back baby sneezes—a congestion threepeat. The noises kept waking me up, like an alarm clock snooze function. She'd stop sneezing just long enough for me to fall back to sleep and then BAM! *Aaaa-choooo! Aaaa-choooo! Aaaa-choooo!* She'd go off again.

At this point, the only part of my body that had consistently stayed asleep was my leg, which had been suffering from a lack of blood circulation for so long that doctors would probably have to amputate it. In my sleep-deprived delirium, I began to wonder if the benefits of losing a leg (primo parking spots, cutting the time you take to clip your toenails in half, being able to sleep without

---

[1] He also drank milk.

your leg falling asleep, etc.) outweigh the downsides (having to use your golf clubs to hold you up instead of using them to hit golf balls absurdly far into the woods).

As I tried to wiggle my leg loose to wake it up, I noticed that my daughter was stuck to me. You read that right: Stuck to me. A thick layer of snot had escaped from her face and penetrated my skin, gluing us together like a grade-school art project. I tried to separate us, but it was no use. I tried to call for help but her head was still pushed deep into my neck, allowing only but a faint whisper to escape. To make matters worse, the TV was on in the background and it was showing my favorite infomercial about the car wax that protects your vehicle so well you can set it on fire and it *still* won't damage the paint—and I couldn't see it!

Clearly, my only option was to wait until my wife woke up in the morning and came down to find us, which she did. She used some warm water to wash away the globs of snot and slowly pull us apart, like a doctor carefully separating conjoined twins.

"Did you give her any baby Tylenol for her fever?"

"We can do that?"

"That's what I said to you when you were getting out of bed."

"I thought you asked me for a Hot Pocket."

"Why would I ask you for a Hot Pocket in the middle of the night?"

"Because they are delicious."

She handed me back my daughter who, by this point, had opened her eyes. She sat on my lap as content as a butterfly. Her nose had stopped leaking down her face and her sneeze button had been switched to the off position. She looked up at me, as if to acknowledge that I played a good game and gave it my all. Then she smiled. After a night of tossing and turning, of sneezing and snotting, of neckaches and blood circulation problems, I was rewarded with a smile. It was the best "thank you" I had ever received.

I celebrated with a breakfast Hot Pocket.

ELEVEN SIGNS THAT YOU NEED TO CALL A DOCTOR

Not all nights are as simple as snuggling on the couch with your daughter. Occasionally, you will actually need to call a doctor. Like most men, I generally prefer to avoid going to any physician for two main reasons:

1. Doctors costs money.
2. I'm super cheap.

When you have a daughter, though, and she's not feeling well, it takes every muscle in your body *not* to call the doctor when she coughs or sneezes or blinks a little too hard. Too many scenarios run through your mind.

Is it an infection?

West Nile?

Is she allergic to our high-definition television? If so, how will we choose whom to keep?

Unless you have a medical degree (or have watched enough *Grey's Anatomy* reruns), it's safe to say that you are no better equipped to diagnose her illness than you are to fly a plane.[2] In fact, even if you wanted to use the website WebMD to diagnose her, you wouldn't be able to, because you are so filled with panic you can't control your fingers long enough to type in her symptoms. Ironically, this is a medical condition that WebMD refers to as "Delirious Dad Syndrome."

While you want to get to the bottom of her illness, you certainly don't want to be calling the doctor over something as minor as the sniffles. That's why I've consulted pediatricians, medical journals,

---

[2]Unless you are a pilot, in which case, this is a really bad analogy.

Oprah, and everyone on Twitter to come up with a list of the top eleven signs that it's worth calling a doctor:

1. Sign #1: Her forehead is hotter than a major league baseball player on a thirty-game hitting streak.
2. Sign #2: She accidentally cut herself and it's too big to be covered up by any of the Princess Band-Aids in your medicine cabinet.
3. Sign #3: She's starting to look a little bit too much like your father-in-law, mainly because of the snot mustache that has formed on her upper lip.
4. Sign #4: Her hair is falling out. No, wait, that's *your* hair falling out onto her. Still, better to call the doctor and make sure your balding problem is not contagious.
5. Sign #5: I'm not sure what the technical term is for this, but her skin starts looking "splotchy."
6. Sign #6: She isn't interested in watching *SportsCenter* with you. (This could be the most serious symptom of them all!)
7. Sign #7: She's been throwing up all day, and no matter how much bacon you feed her she still won't stop ralphing.
8. Sign #8: You attempt to give her a classic high-five and she walks right by you without even acknowledging it.[3]
9. Sign #9: She fell off a step and now her knee bends in multiple directions.
10. Sign #10: She lies on the couch lethargically, only getting up to pee and to complain that *Dora the Explorer* has "really jumped the shark."
11. Sign #11: She says that mom's hugs are more soothing than your hugs. Obviously she's delirious and needs immediate medical attention. Skip the doctor and head straight for the ER. We can only hope that it's not too late.

---

[3]It is possible that she mistook your attempt to high-five her for a wave. May want to test again with a rock bump.

WHY DAUGHTERS NEED DADS WHEN THEY ARE SICK

Once you have a daughter, it is 100 percent guaranteed that you will overreact every time she gets sick—and that's okay. Daughters actually *need* dads to overreact. They count on us to overreact. It's part of the healing process. Medicine and doctors and Band-Aids can provide only so much relief, but a dad can give daughters something no modern medicine can: Someone to hold them close and assure them everything will be fine.

One caveat to mention: Be sure to invest in a DVR, as daughters almost exclusively get sick during March Madness, the Super Bowl, and other extremely important sports championships. I think it's a daughter's special way of telling you that she loves you. It's also her way of telling you to turn on *Dora*.

Despite her poor timing, your job is quite simple: Hug her when she needs it. Feed her comfort food when what she needs is to feel comfortable. Be willing to injure yourself if it gets her to laugh and forget about the pain, even if only for a few moments.[4] The faster you can recover from the idea of your little princess being sick, the faster she will likely recover from actually being sick.

And, if you're lucky, when that flu has disappeared from her sinuses and she's up and about, running around and playing like the daughter you've grown to love, she'll put on her toy stethoscope and tend to you as you lay in bed, battling the flu she gave you. It's her way of saying "Thank you, Dad" and "I love you, Dad" all at once.

Whatever you do, though, don't let her take your temperature. I've seen where my daughters put their thermometer on their dolls and I can tell you, it ain't in the mouth.

---

[4] I highly recommend pretending to trip and fall on the floor. You may not even have to pretend if her toys are lying about as they normally are.

Chapter 10

Diaper-to-Bathroom Breakdown

(THIS CHAPTER STINKS)

When other dads talk about their own daughters, they often only describe the perks, like squeezing their adorable cheeks and using them to practice ventriloquism. (If you haven't tried this yet, you must. It's utterly hilarious and a hit at afternoon barbeques.) They tell you that the minute that baby girl falls asleep on your chest, you are given a free pass from your wife to nap right along with them—and it's true! (The sight of a daddy with his girl asleep on him is impossible for a woman to resist.) They also tell you that your mom will be so thankful you gave her a granddaughter that she'll forgive you for that one time you accidentally set the rug on fire. Ah, the perks.

What they never talk about are the two dirtiest terms in the history of fatherhood: diapers and potty training. The foul, disgusting, awfulness of diapers and the miserable, frustrating, mind-numbing experience of potty training. This is the information you need that no one is willing to give you. So read this chapter with caution— but be sure to read it—as I'm going to dive right in and give you the inside scoop on why it's important to give it your all and why you desperately need to keep your mother's number on speed dial.

ANATOMY 101

Newsflash: Daughters have different plumbing than we do and, from the moment they are born, they will use it to pee all over you. And no, I'm not talking metaphorically.[1]

For the first couple years of her life, your daughter will use a diaper. A diaper is like a small toga that wraps around her private zone and absorbs all fluids and solids, but not gases. It generally has some cute brand name on it like Huggies or Pampers or Luvs, none of which are accurate descriptions of the relationship you

---

[1] Mainly because I don't know what "metaphorically" means.

will have with diapers. Most important, these diapers have adhesive straps on the sides that will stick to your arm hair and cause you great pain.

Changing a diaper isn't all that hard, so long as you have six hands. That's why many couples will refer to diaper changing as a "team sport" and will try to recruit as many people as they can. You need:

1. One hand to hold the dirty diaper
2. One hand to hold her legs to keep her from squirming around in her business
3. One hand to hold her arms and keep her from sticking her hands in her business
4. One hand to wipe everything that needs to be wiped[2]
5. One hand to put on the new diaper
6. One hand to hold in the vomit from the awful stench

I remember the first time I ever changed a diaper. We were still in the hospital, waiting for the fine cuisine that is hospital food to be delivered to our room, when my eldest daughter dropped her first load (which happened to look a lot like the fine cuisine that is hospital food).

"Don't worry, I've got this," I said.

I proceeded to undo the diaper, wipe up the considerable mess, and put the new diaper on, all in a record time of 22 minutes. (Top that, hot shot!) I held her up, proud as a papa can be. I smiled at my wife and said, "See, I'm going to make a great dad." She smiled back at me.

"You put the diaper on backwards."

---

[2]It's okay if it takes you seventy-five baby wipes to clean off your daughter's bottom, even if it takes your wife only one. In most sports, that's a score of 75–1 and would be considered winning.

THE FIVE LEVELS OF DIRTY DIAPERS (AND HOW TO SURVIVE THEM)

Not all dirty diapers are created equal. Some contain big messes. Some are small. Some stay dry for hours upon hours. Others need to be replaced within minutes of putting them on. Thankfully, the government has created the Dirty Diaper Threat Level Alert System, which allows you to gauge and properly prepare yourself for what's to come. This system is designed to help you diagnose the potential threat of each type of dirty diaper and advise on how to prepare for (and handle) each situation. No need to thank me for sharing this information yet—thank me after you've survived a Code Red.[3]

Level 1: Code Green

This condition is declared when smell is minimal or nonexistent and there is a low risk of bodily fluids escaping the diaper. In other words, she's just wet. Federal departments, as well as your immediate household, should consider taking the following general protective measures:

1. Keep wipes and spare diapers close by.
2. Make sure a changing pad is laid out somewhere away from foot traffic.
3. Take off old diaper; put on new diaper.
4. Dispose of diaper in any garbage can that happens to also be on your way to whichever fridge holds the cold beer.

---

[3] I am well aware that I didn't mention a Code Erupting Volcano, but the details of that are even too gruesome for me to print in this book. Plus, I like knowing you still have one surprise to look forward to.

Level 2: Code Blue

Also known as "a Stinker," this condition is declared when there is no actual evidence of an explosion, but there is a general risk of your daughter dropping a load based on the terrible smell of her flatulance. Code Blue farts are toxic and can kill. I've seen a Code Blue take the lives of two doll babies, a Cabbage Patch Kid, and one unsuspecting Mr. Potato Head. Consider taking the following general protective measures:

1. Use latex gloves to slowly peek in the diaper to make sure there's nothing actually in there. If there is, you may have to declare a Code Yellow or Orange (see following).
2. Remove smell by opening windows or cutting off your nose.
3. Invite mother-in-law over for dinner, but only if she can arrive in next four minutes. Hand off baby, run out to pick up pizza. Wait until she's addressed the forthcoming Code Yellow or Code Orange before returning. Important Note: Don't forget to use $2-off pizza coupon.

Level 3: Code Yellow

A Code Yellow is declared when the diaper is filled with a bomb but remains contained. Signs of a Code Yellow include sweating, grunting, crying, and foul odors—and that's just from you. The baby, likely embarrassed that she had to drop one in front of everyone in the living room, will pretend like nothing happened. Consider taking the following general protective measures:

1. Also pretend like nothing happened.

Level 4: Code Orange

Any diaper that contains poop mixed with visible, unharmed bonus objects is considered a Code Orange. Bonus objects that can appear in a diaper include—but are not limited to—the following: berries, corn, peas, nickels, bottle caps, missing remote control buttons, craps dice (pun intended) or tiny lightbulbs (it's as if her butt had a great idea!). A Code Orange offers plenty of surprises and is jokingly referred to by your mother and mother-in-law as a "gift basket." (NOTE: Never accept a "gift basket" from your mother or mother-in-law.)

This is the type of diaper you offer to change because:

1. It's not lethal.
2. It's not messy.
3. It's likely you'll find your missing car keys.

Consider taking the following general protective measures, though:

1. Take off favorite sports jersey.
2. Put on surgical mask.
3. Sing "We Are the Champions" by Queen to pump you up.
4. Make sure someone's purse is close and open. Dirty diaper + Open purse = practical joke enjoyed by all.

Level 5: Code Red

In some parts of the country, this is known as a "Code Brown" or a "Nuclear Attack." Slimy particles not only escape from her diaper, they leap and ruin anything within a five-mile radius. Liked that onesie? Too bad, it's got poop on it. Liked that Green Day poster on your wall? Too bad, it's got poop on it. Liked your forehead? Too bad, it's got poop on it. Liked that sixty-two-inch flat screen TV? Too bad ... well, actually, you were wise enough to cover it in eleven layers of plastic and four rolls of duct tape to protect it during just such an event. Good for you! Consider taking the following general protective measures:

1. Locate your Hazmat suit.
2. Pray for a saint to arrive and change the diaper instead of you.
3. Man up and change that diaper, no matter what is clinging to your forehead.
4. Take picture and send to your wife while she is at work. She will appreciate it.
5. And finally, place all material that's fallen victim to a Code Red in a garbage bag, seal tightly, drive to neighboring state, and bury it in the backyard of a Cubs fan. (Another practical joke enjoyed by all.)

PHASE 2: POTTY TRAINING

The good news: She won't wear diapers forever.

The bad news: One day, your little angel will be ready to move on to a lengthy, painful operation known as "Potty Training." This will be brought on by one of five factors:

1. Your daughter shows interest in the potty.
2. Your wife says it's time to start potty training.
3. Your mother-in-law says it's time to start potty training (and then passive-aggressively brings it up over and over and over again).
4. Your wife's friends say that their favorite mommy blogger says it's time to start potty training.
5. Your daughter is now ten years old. You've failed as a parent.

Potty training is one of the trickier elements of having a daughter, particularly because everyone will offer you oodles and oodles of unsolicited advice and absolutely none of it will work. Person after person will tell you her success story, especially your mother-in-law, who will claim that she had your wife potty trained by the age of three months. (NOTE: You'll become suspect of her timeline when, at three months of age, the only thing your daughter is trained to do is drool.)

Step 1: Bribery

Recommendations on how to transition your daughter from diapers to the potty will range from "just let her pee in underwear for a couple of days until it bothers her" to "set an alarm clock and put her on the potty every hour" to "just let your wife handle it." Perhaps these methods will work for you, but they certainly didn't for me. My daughter was too stubborn. Which is why I had to do what I do best: I bribe.

"All right, sweetie, it's time to go potty."

"But I don't want to go potty."

"If you pee on the potty, I'll give you an M&M."

"What color?"

"Green."

"I don't like green."

"What color do you like?"

"Pink."

"I don't think we have any that are pink. What about a red?"

"RED IS NOT PINK!"

(As punishment for suggesting that it was, she gives you a look that lets you know she's contemplating pooping in her pants.)

"Daddy pees on the potty. Why can't you?"

"What if the toilet monster comes up and bites my butt?"

"There's no such thing as a toilet monster."

"Sure there is, Daddy. Mommy was upset the other day when she went to go potty. Said you left a toilet monster in there."

"Oh. Well, what she meant was . . . never mind what she meant. If you go potty, I'll play dress up with you. How does that sound?"

"No, thanks. You don't make a very pretty princess."

"If you don't go potty on the potty, then I'm never taking you to grandma's house ever again!"

"That's okay, I'll just have mommy take me."

Similar conversations took place over the course of about five months and slowly drove me to alcoholism. Just kidding. (The Cincinnati Reds bullpen of the early 2000s drove me to alcoholism.) I begged and pleaded and threatened and rewarded and nothing seemed to work. My daughter just refused to take that leap.

Step 2: Give Up

So, I did what any other guy would do at this point: I gave up. I came to grips with the fact that she would be in diapers for the rest of her life. Then a funny thing happened.

We were at my friend's house and his daughter, a bit older than mine, peed on the potty. In an effort to be like the older friend she adored, my daughter asked if she could go on the potty too. And she did! It was a miracle, right up there with the U.S. hockey team defeating the Russians in the 1980 Olympics and the popularity of Justin Bieber's hair! All it took was a little peer pressure from a friend to get things rolling. From then on, she just told me when she had to go to the potty and I'd put her on.

And that evening before bed, she got on that potty and dropped something that I'd been hoping she'd do for the past five months.

Her first toilet monster. And I couldn't have been any prouder.

PUBLIC RESTROOMS: THE UNDER-NO-CIRCUMSTANCES LIST

Once your daughter is potty trained, it's inevitable that your wife will make a poor decision and let you take your daughter out in public without her. She may let you do something simple, like take your daughter to the grocery store, or something complicated, like take your daughter to the grocery store with the intent to buy something. Either way, it's guaranteed that your daughter will have to go to the bathroom at least eleven times—even if she went just before you left the house.

Seems like it shouldn't be a problem, considering:

1. She is potty trained.
2. You understand how to operate a toilet.

Wrong! There is a giant problem—and it isn't that you forgot your wallet at home and won't realize this fact until you've loaded your cart with more than $200 worth of groceries. The problem is that your wife, who absolutely hates public restrooms, has threatened your life if you don't follow her "Under-No-Circumstances List." It's a fairly straightforward, yet very specific, list of how you are to conduct yourself and care for your daughter in any public restroom scenario. If you learn nothing else from this book, learn this list. Your life may depend on it.

The list is as follows.

Under no circumstances are you to:

1. Take your daughter into a public restroom without first making sure that there are no shifty-looking people in there, like drug addicts or Steve Buscemi.

2. Let your daughter's posterior (this is fancy talk for "hiney") touch the toilet seat.[4]
3. Allow her underwear or pants to touch the floor.
4. Allow her feet to touch the floor.
5. Allow her feet to come within twelve inches of the floor.
6. Allow her to touch any wall, door, or sink, or anything else that is located within the public restroom, other than you.
7. Grant her the authority to flush the toilet. This must be done by you and with your foot. If you use your hands, you are no longer allowed to touch anything in the house, including your wife.
8. Let your daughter make eye contact with anyone in the restroom.
9. Ever let her use one of those reusable hand-drying towel thingys that hang from the wall. If there are no other options, let her dry her hands on your sleeve.
10. Authorize her to go to the bathroom by herself.
11. Talk about the bathroom experience with your wife, who is already grossed out just thinking about public restrooms.
12. Go to a public restroom and have a stress-free experience ever again.

So . . . How Does It Work, Then?

Fact: Your wife has made it absolutely clear that under no circumstances are you to let your daughter sit directly on the toilet seat of a public restroom. So what do you do when you and your daughter are out in a public place, like an IHOP or the casino, and she has to pee? Here are four acceptable techniques:

---

[4]Whatever you do, don't say, "Well, I wiped the toilet off before I sat her on the seat." This will lead to an automatic suspension of any and all sexy time with your wife for at least three months.

1. **"The Layering System":** Use a minimum of two rolls of toilet paper to layer the seat first, then put napkins over that, then put your shirt on top of that. Set her gently on top of the mountain you've built and pray she doesn't fall in.
2. **"The Hover":** Hold her over the seat by placing one arm under her knees and the other around her back, and watch as she confidently pees out of the toilet and onto your shoes.
3. **"The Sink Method":** Avoid nasty toilet seats all together by letting your daughter squat in the sink. This plan of attack is only acceptable when no one is looking or when the sink is the only "stall" that doesn't have someone sleeping in it.
4. **"The Make Her Pee Standing Up Like Her Dad Plan":** If it's good enough for dudes . . .

I BELIEVE IN YOU!

Now I know what you're thinking: *I am never going to survive this diaper and potty training stuff.* But I am walking proof that no matter how talentless you are, no matter how little confidence you have, no matter how scared you are to get poop on your arm, you will make it. You have to. Your daughter needs you to survive and teach her how to do so many important things in life, like how to drive a stick shift and how to eat fifty blazing-hot buffalo wings in one sitting without a drink. She also needs you to show her how you persevered though all the Code Red dirty diapers and the months of potty training and the pains of awkwardly trying to hold her over the public restroom toilet seats without letting any part of her body touch anything—in other words, one of the most challenging times of your life—only to come out on top. It's your drive and determination that will ultimately fuel her ambition to be the best that she can be, whether it's a doctor, a lawyer, a softball player, or a ballerina. And when she walks up on that

Harvard stage at her college graduation, giving her valedictorian speech to the crowd of thousands, you'll lean back and listen as she thanks you for your love, for your support, and for letting her flush that public restroom toilet that one time, even though "Mom said not to."

Duck and cover: Your wife is coming for you.

Chapter 11

How to Get Her to Choose Sports Over Ballet

(THE PLAYBOOK)

So far I've walked you through tea parties, Dora, Disney, dealing with public restrooms, pink wardrobe problems, and more. They are territories that I've been through. They are territories that all dads who have daughters have been through or will go through. On the surface they are awful, but once you dive in, they are only *kind of* awful. And, truthfully, you may start to enjoy most of these things with your daughter (during *SportsCenter* commercial breaks, I often flip on Dora and dream about cuddling with my sweet little girls on the couch).

It's important to remember that all of these things, while difficult, won't kill you.

However, ballet will kill you.

THE ALLURE OF BALLET

Before your daughter can even walk, every female that comes in contact with her will assume she is going to take ballet. They will buy her itty bitty ballerina shoes, ballerina-themed outfits, ballerina toys and costumes, and mention (quite frequently) how much they all loved taking ballet when they were young (which is a lie). Your mother-in-law will break out videos of your wife as a little girl dancing in something called "a recital," which I believe is slang for "the most painful thing you will ever watch." This should be a federal crime. Unfortunately, according to the U.S. Judicial System, it is not.[1]

WHAT IS BALLET, ANYWAY?

Ballet consists of (what else?) pink uniforms (which my wife and daughter refer to as *leotards*), none of which have numbers or

---

[1] If you ever run for Congress and support banning all ballet recitals, you have my vote.

team names on them, and evening practices that conflict with your already jam-packed schedule of grilling, eating, and squashing bugs that have made their way into your basement. It also consists of two dozen girls lined up, trying to do the same dance moves at the same time, and failing miserably. (In their defense, most of these girls come from a long line of rhythm-challenged dads who couldn't synchronize a head-bob if their hairline depended on it.[2]) Worse yet, there are no halftimes or seventh-inning stretches.

To top it off, ballet alters the continuum of time and creates a special "ballet hour," which is much longer than a standard hour. How much longer? Let me break it down in this simple equation and in terms you will understand:

$$\text{Standard hour} = 60 \text{ minutes}$$
$$\text{Ballet hour} = 4{,}440 \text{ times the number of minutes in a standard hour}$$
$$60 \text{ minutes} \times 4440 \text{ times} =$$
$$\text{the approximate length of any Sandra Bullock movie}$$

The financial burden ballet places on your family is enough to give you a heart attack. It's enough to give the government a heart attack. Between the classes, clothes, shoes (which rival the cost of a brand-new Mustang), gas to get her to and from, and bribery animals,[3] you're looking at thousands of dollars in expenses. And unless there's a sudden demand for something you have in excess, like bellybutton lint or back hair, you'll probably have to get a second job. Of course, you'll have to make sure the hours don't conflict with ballet practice.

---

[2] Not my girls, though. I totally rock on the dance floor.
[3] Bribery animals are what you purchase to bribe your daughter so she won't tell your wife that you left ballet practice to play blackjack at the casino.

EXACTLY HOW BAD IS IT?

As you can see, ballet is painful. Super painful. I don't think you realize quite how painful it is. To demonstrate, I'm going to give you a list of ten things I'd rather have happen to me than attend a ballet recital:

1. Get head-butted in the crotch.
2. Have my hair set on fire (or, at least, what is left of my hair).
3. Eat a turkey sandwich only to discover that it isn't turkey and instead is the flesh of Jar Jar Binks.
4. Be forced to listen to Carly Rae Jepsen's classic "Call Me Maybe" on repeat . . . forever.
5. Be caught buying tampons for my wife by my college buddies.
6. Be caught buying tampons for my wife by my college buddies *and* by my sports hero, Hall of Fame shortstop Barry Larkin.
7. Have a naked picture of me go viral on the Internet. (Though this would be a win for the Internet.)
8. Find out that I'm growing a tail.
9. Get stuck in traffic only to realize that I have four pots of coffee in me—and a small bladder.
10. Three words: Alien Anal Probe.

Taking all of this into account, you can see why it is essential that you do everything in your power to steer your daughter away from ballet and into something more constructive and entertaining, such as bowling or cutting the grass. Better yet, set her on a path toward athletics so she stands a sporting chance (pun totally intended!) at participating in something that you could cheer her on throughout the years (while wearing one of those giant foam fingers that you love) and could also one day land her a multi-million-dollar contract—thus, taking care of you and helping you fulfill your lifelong dream of swimming in a giant pile of money like Scrooge McDuck.

Dad Lesson

Tailgating before a ballet recital is frowned upon. Flasks are not, mainly because they are kept hidden in your pocket, away from those with frowny faces. Keep yours filled at all times. No matter how hard you try to avoid it, you never know when a ballet recital is going to sneak up on you.

THE PLAYBOOK: SEVEN WAYS TO TRAIN YOUR DAUGHTER TO SUBCONSCIOUSLY CHOOSE SPORTS OVER BALLET

Convincing your daughter that ballet is more evil than Judas and that sports are holier than Jesus doesn't happen overnight. No, sir. It's a delicate process that takes years of planning and requires complete dedication. Unfortunately for me (but thankfully for you), I've gone through the process three times now so I've developed a sure-fire plan to help you train your daughter to choose sports over dancing in a unitard. These tactics *will* work if applied correctly. Here they are:

Tactic #1: Audio Assimilation

Instead of turning on a music box when you put her to bed (which screams "make me a ballerina"), turn on a radio and have her fall asleep listening to your favorite baseball team's game. In the winter, have her listen to the football game of the week. This will train her mind to dream less about twinkling her toes and more about sliding hard into second to break up the double play.

No game on? No problem. Compose a playlist of the most storied moments from your favorite sporting events (like Pete Rose's record-breaking hit or Lou Gehrig's "Luckiest Man" speech, or the entire script of *Hoosiers*) and have it queued up, ready to play when needed.

Tactic #2: Get Equipment for Her Dolls

Buy tiny baseball gloves for all of her dolls and, when you help her play with them, pretend they are playing catch. NOTE: She may, from time to time, confuse the gloves with oven mitts. Don't panic. Just start acting like you are tossing the food back and forth, and tack the word "ball" onto the end of everything ("Hey sweetie, toss that potato-ball over to me. I'm going to toss this watermelon-ball back to you").

Tactic #3: Create Olfactory Associations

Any time there is a dancing show on television, put something incredibly stinky in the room. This will train her to associate a foul smell with any type of professional dance, making her less likely to want to do it. There are many things that can accomplish the stink necessary to pull this off: a pile of sweaty gym socks, a dead fish hidden on the mantle, an open diaper behind the television, etc. I prefer to stick with the simplest yet most effective of them all, bean farts.

Tactic #4: Teachable Moments

Describe all mathematical equations in sporting terms. "So dear, if you have seven points from a touchdown and add three points from a field goal, how many points do you have?" When she gets the answer correct, give her a high-five and then bump chests.

Tactic #5: Movie Makeover

Replace all her Disney movies with *Field of Dreams*.[4]

---

[4]Except for *Tangled*. That movie is pretty badass.

Tactic #6: Introduce the Classics

If she asks for a bedtime story, read her *The New Bill James Historical Baseball Abstract*. This will not only help her appreciate the value of sporting statistics, it might also coincidentally put her to sleep.

Tactic #7: Bribery

Offer to give her a cookie if she promises to do anything even remotely athletic.

These tactics are 100 percent guaranteed to work, unless you have a wife who is smarter than you (and let's face it, we all have wives who are smarter than us) and she continues to paint pictures of sweet ballerinas dancing in your daughter's dreams. There's very little that can stop this influence. You can threaten not to put-out, but she knows this is a total bluff (and you are probably already trying to seduce her before you finish uttering the threat). You can try to use the phrase "I put my foot down." If you're lucky, it'll work. If you're unlucky, she'll put her foot down too—but it ain't gonna be on the floor.

Your only hope is to continue to fight the good fight, giving it your all and making sure you do everything in your power—when talking to your daughter—to make ballet sound about as appealing as broccoli-flavored ice cream.

If your daughter still isn't deterred, do what I do: cry.

WHAT HAPPENS WHEN YOUR DAUGHTER STILL WANTS TO TAKE BALLET

No matter how hard you try, some daughters are just destined to take ballet. You could line up all the soccer balls in the world in front of her and she'd just dance in and out of them on her tiptoes, without even accidentally bumping one with her feet. You'll plead with her and beg her not to do it, but when her mind's made up, her mind is made up.

"Daddy, I really want to take ballet."

"Are you sure?"

"I'm really, really sure."

"If you agree not to take ballet, I'll let you drive the car."

"My feet don't reach the pedals, Daddy."

"On a scale of one-to-ten princesses, with one princess meaning you have no interest in ballet and ten princesses meaning you wish you could take ballet every night, where do you fall?"

"I'd say one hundred princesses!"

You faint in disbelief.

"But that's because I really love princesses . . . and ballet."

You can attempt to discuss this with your wife, but she will immediately take your daughter's side without even considering your concerns.

"Listen, there is no way I want her to take ballet."

"She's taking ballet."

"But ballet is awful."

"She's taking ballet."

"But I've already invested $4,000 in top-of-the-line softball equipment!"

"She's . . . wait, you *what?*"

"Did I say 'softball equipment'? I meant 'college.'"

"If she wants to take ballet, she's taking ballet."

"If you agree to ban her from taking ballet, I will agree to rub your feet every night for the rest of my life."

"If I wanted you to rub my feet, you would rub my feet."

"Oh yeah, how is that?"

She gives you that seductive smile that makes all the blood rush out of your brain and into your other brain.

"Ugh. How often will I have to take her to ballet?"

"Every night—after you've finished rubbing my feet."

Once it's clear that your daughter is taking ballet and there is absolutely nothing you can do to stop it, there are only two actions left for you to consider: ritual suicide or acceptance. Both have their pros and cons, but in the end, acceptance is the better choice.[5]

Dad Lesson

Now that you are a Ballet Dad, you must dress like a Ballet Dad. Mandatory apparel for all Ballet Dads include a windbreaker, track pants, neon-colored see-through visor, oversized sunglasses, tri-colored tube socks, and loafers. Carefully sculpted facial hair is not required, but is highly encouraged.

HOW TO BE A BALLET DAD IN A SOCCER MOM WORLD

Earlier in this chapter, I mentioned that ballet will kill you, which is true. But you can slow down the process (and potentially stop it) by not only accepting ballet into your daughter's life, but also embracing it. Don't just drive her to and from classes, sitting in "Dad Row" playing games on your smartphone and trying to avoid the class instructor, who will engage the first person who makes eye contact with her into a long conversation about the history of pliés.[6] Instead, try these methods for embracing your fate:

1. Become the biggest ballet fan there ever was, cheering on your daughter as if it were the bottom of the ninth, two outs, game on the line, and she stepped up to the plate.

---

[5]Barely.

[6]Fun fact: "*Plié*" is a French term meaning "to bend." In ballet, there are two basic types of pliés: a *demi-plié*, where you bend your knees ever so slightly as if you were trying to field a grounder that took a bad hop, and a *grand plié*, where you point your knees out and squat as if you were trying to take a dump in the woods.

"YOU CAN DO IT, SWEETIE! I BELIEVE IN YOU!"

2. Whenever she finishes a dance, you stand and clap louder than all the other parents combined. Bring the camera *and* camcorder so you can document in multiple mediums.

3. Hire an artist to sit by your side and capture your daughter's big moment in oils.

4. Have a button made with her picture on it and pin it to your shirt, wearing it to every ballet event (the bigger the button, the better!).

5. Search "glossary of ballet" online and learn every term possible so you can talk ballet with your daughter, just like you'd talk football schematics with a drinking buddy. "Oh, man, that was one hellava grand jeté, sweetie. Your feet positions were spot on and you really nailed that soutenu en tournant! If the teacher would just add a pas de chat to the routine, your team would win the championship!"

Okay, so I have absolutely no idea if there are ballet competitions or a world ballet championship, but if there were, I'd want my daughter to strive to get there no matter how many ballet hours I had to sit through. And I'd root her on every step of the way, big foam fingers and all.

Chapter 12

How to Deal with Her First Crush

(THIS IS NO TIME FOR JOKES)

Shotgun.

Next chapter.

I'm just kidding. (Maybe.) In fact, it's important to recognize early on that you can't rely solely on the shotgun. Having a daughter is all about thinking long term and laying groundwork to make sure she can grow up to be a smart, happy, healthy adult woman who loathes all men except for her dad. You can set rules, such as she is not allowed to date until after she is married (and even then, all dates require parental supervision for the first five years). But it's possible she won't abide by these types of rules and will start dating some knucklehead in high school anyway. That's why it's super important that you take a pre-emptive stand.

ESTABLISH YOUR REPUTATION NOW

These early formative years are delicate, not just for your daughter but for all the boys who will surround your daughter at the playground, at daycare, at school, at Disney on Ice, etc. Addressing the issue now, many years before boys start acting like knuckleheads, is key to putting them in their place and letting them know how intimidating you are. I recommend writing a carefully worded boilerplate letter that you can carry with you at all times and leave at a moment's notice. You never know where you will be when your daughter mentions a boy's name (which is the first sign that a crush is forming), so it's important to be prepared. That way, you can find out where he lives and glue the letter to his bedroom door.[1]

---

[1]Leaving a drop or two of blood on the letter isn't necessary, but is a nice touch if you feel so inclined.

I know writing a letter like this is tough and time consuming. If you don't have time to write your own, you can use mine. I've included it below.

A Letter to Any Boy Your Daughter Shows Interest In

Dear Knucklehead,

Have you ever heard of the Dad Fairy? No? Well, let me explain.

It has been brought to my attention that my daughter has taken an interest in you. While this may sound pleasant at first, I can promise you, it is not a pleasant thing. In fact, and I'll be quite frank with you, it's probably the worst thing that will happen to you in your lifetime (unless your parents are Cubs fans, then *that* is probably the worst thing that will happen in your lifetime—but this is a close second).

It's important that you know how much my daughter means to me. I would give up everything I own, including my house, my car, my autographed Boomer Esiason jersey, my freezer full of pork that I bought on mega sale (and the only thing I love more than pork is mega sales), my collection of bobbleheads, my Highest-Score-of-the-Week Men's Division 4 Beer League bowling trophy, my fifty-two-inch HDTV, and my own kidneys just to make sure she's okay. Nothing is more important to me. So when I see a potential problem, I get angry.

Red Alert: You are a potential problem.

When I get angry I turn into the Dad Fairy. Sure, it sounds like a cute character from *Pinocchio* who you'd want to take home and snuggle with while reading a nice book. But the Dad Fairy isn't pleasant. He lurks quietly in the shadows until he is set off by a knucklehead, such as yourself, turning into a full-blown madman whom I can't control.[2] He is so violent that he blacks out with rage and, when he awakens, is covered head-to-toe in blood and is carrying freshly ripped-out bones. This action is commonly referred to as "Beast Mode" and is brought on by boys who so much as even glance at his daughter. He looks like a combination of a vampire, a werewolf, a zombie, and Thor. He is scary and unpredictable and you don't want to meet him.

I know what you're thinking: *What do I have to worry about? I don't like girls. They are dumb and stupid and full of cooties. I'd rather shove a crayon up my nose than like a girl.* This is what all knuckleheads think. Play dumb all you want. Pull their pigtails to try to prove your disinterest. It's not fooling anyone, especially me. I've seen the way you share your paste with all the girls in preschool, including my daughter. This is the type of thing that causes the Dad Fairy to pay a visit to your home in the middle of the night.

If you value your life, you will heed my advice: Transfer to someplace where it's a little harder for you to see my daughter, such as a nice boarding school in Uzbekistan. If, for some reason, Uzbekistan won't take you, I suggest mysteriously coming down with an extreme case of the chicken pox that will render you unable to attend class and cause you to miss the rest of the school year. Anything short of that will put your life in jeopardy.

Should you not listen to me and, instead, continue to see my daughter on a regular basis, take note: I, the Dad Fairy, *WILL* come for you. Could be today. Could be tomorrow. Could be yesterday. (That's right, knucklehead, I can time travel.[3]) Could be when you most expect it. Could be when you least expect it. But I'm coming. And I'm in Beast Mode.

---

[2]Nice use of "whom"!
[3]You can't time travel, but he doesn't have to know that.

Oh, and in case you can't read yet, I've decided to draw you a diagram to make sure we are clear on this:

Remember: The Tooth Fairy takes teeth and leaves money. The Dad Fairy takes teeth and leaves broken bones.

Stay away from my daughter.

Sincerely,
Mr. Your Worst Nightmare

This letter is guaranteed to put the fear of God in him. Or make him wet his pants.[4] This effort, while incredibly valuable, is only the first step in what will become a lifetime battle to keep your little girl from growing up and being hounded by boys. Cherish every moment you have before that battle turns into a war, which I hear happens around the teenage years.

Dad Lesson

If there is a particular boy that all of the girls (including your daughter) seem to have a crush on, immediately notify all the other dads. This allows you time to work as a team and build a game plan on how to properly "rid" yourselves of this "problem." It also allows you time to form a secret club where you can talk, commiserate, and admit—in complete confidence—that you are starting to like the color pink.

---

[4]Sure, he'll "claim" it's because he's not potty trained yet, but we both know the truth.

Chapter 13

Future Bankruptcy

(HOW TO START SAVING
FOR THAT WEDDING)

In your "predaughter" years, your bank account probably housed many dollar bills that were earmarked for the three Bs: beer, bachelor parties, and bacon. You'd spend as you'd see fit, living by the phrase "carpe diem!" which, when translated from Latin to English, means "double down!" You'd take your wife to a romantic dinner and a movie, splurging for the biggest popcorn and sodas the theater concession stand had to offer. Heck, you even tipped the guy who took your ticket, just because you could.

Not anymore.

WHERE YOUR MONEY GOES NOW

Raising a daughter is the second most expensive thing you will ever be responsible for, just after your cable bill. Daughters require a lot of maintenance (and by "maintenance" I mean "shoes") and attention (and by "attention" I mean "more shoes"). They also need an extraordinary amount of clothes. Summer clothes, winter clothes, fall clothes, birthday party clothes, visiting Grandma and Grandpa clothes, bedtime clothes, vacation clothes, etc. And by "etc." I mean a crap-ton of more clothes. Dads aren't used to this, as we still wear the same four T-shirts we've owned since high school. We take pride in this and get disappointed when our wives try to sneak something new into our wardrobe, such as a shirt *without* holes in it.[1]

Clothes and "maintenance" aren't the only additional price tags that come with a girl. Girls require not only shampoo but also *conditioner. Conditioner!* You make sacrifices, such as going bald, to help cut beauty product costs, while she's adding expensive hair products, such as *conditioner*, to raise them! Unbelievable! Girls also need at least one princess dress that fits to go along with one

---

[1] Holes in T-shirts are known as "character." They also provide an excellent breeze on hot summer days.

fairy wand and one tiara—both of which you will step on, break, and have to replace once every four hours.

But none of these expenses compare to the big one. You know, THE big one.

And no, I'm not talking about building that moat around your house.

WEDDING BELLS ARE EXPENSIVE

The most common joke that most folks make when they find out you're having a daughter is this:

"A daughter? You better start saving up for her wedding."

This joke is old, trite, and 100 percent true. Weddings don't grow on trees. Neither do receptions with an open bar. Make all the twenty-first century excuses you want (such as "she can pay for her own wedding"), but from the first time you see her in a princess dress and she gives you a hug, you know you will ultimately pay for whatever she wants. You just desperately hope that what she wants is to become a nun.

That's why you have to start preparing now. If your daughter is still in the womb, you're lucky: you have a few extra months to start saving. If she's already here, snuggling in your arms on the couch, you are at a major disadvantage and need to catch up quickly. But before you start worrying about how to save the money (which I'll explain later), first you must determine *how much* you will need to save.

EARLY SIGNS OF AN EXPENSIVE WEDDING: WEDDING COST INDICATORS

Not all weddings are created equal, and most come with different costs. They range from "super expensive" to "even more super expensive" to "I-now-live-in-a-cardboard-box-because-I-sold-everything-I-own-so-my-daughter-could-have-a-chocolate-fountain-at-her-wedding expensive." The best way to gauge this is by looking out for *Wedding Cost Indicators*. Wedding Cost Indicators are found in the likes and dislikes of your daughter. Let me give you a few examples.

Wedding Cost Indicator Example #1

If your daughter likes to smush all her food together, that's a Wedding Cost Indicator that she is agreeable to buffet-style dining (less expensive). But if she prefers to keep her food separate and is always waiting for you to feed her, that's a Wedding Cost Indicator that she'll want a pricey, formal sit-down dinner—and that you'll also have to hire someone to feed her.

Wedding Cost Indicator Example #2

Your daughter prefers to leave her hair down, hanging around her face, blowing in the wind without a care about how it looks. This is a Wedding Cost Indicator that she won't need to hire some fancy stylist to do her hair and makeup for her wedding. She'll be content with letting a friend do it (dirt cheap). On the other hand, if she's always asking you to put her hair up in pigtails or style it with bows, barrettes, and headbands, you're looking at a hairdresser cost that mirrors your monthly mortgage payment.

Wedding Cost Indicator Example #3

When she talks on her Tinkerbell phone and pretends to have conversations with others, does she:

A. Always call only close family members?
B. Call family members and friends?
C. Call everyone she's ever met, including characters from her favorite Disney movies?

If the answer is A (always call family members), you're in luck, as you may be able to get away with a small gathering and reception with just those closest to you. If the answer is B (call family member and friends), you're probably on the hook for a fairly large wedding where you'll need a giant cake and a DJ who plays songs like "The Electric Slide." If the answer is C, I hope you own Google.

MY (DAUGHTER'S) FIRST WEDDING EXPERIENCE AND WHY IT FREAKED ME OUT

The first time I really noticed Wedding Cost Indicators was when my eldest daughter suddenly wanted to "play wedding." If you haven't had the pleasure of playing wedding yet, congratulations! You've done a fine job hiding the idea of marriage from your daughter and I salute you. But if she ever does figure it out, there are a few things you need to know.

The Groom

First, she chooses a groom from this list of characters: one of her dolls (weird); an imaginary friend (even weirder); a boy from daycare (see Chapter 12); or you, her dad (completely acceptable). Now, I know it sounds odd that she'd choose her dad to be the groom, but this makes perfect sense because:

1. she absolutely loves you
2. you are an important man in her life
3. you are conveniently *present* every time she wants to play wedding.

The Ceremony

Second, you must prepare a reception for after the ceremony. You can often get away with fake glasses of champagne to toast and pretend dinner plates from her Disney princess party collection, but you will need something of substance that will:

1. make her happy
2. not ruin her appetite (this is a rule mandated by your wife).

I recommend Twizzlers—I mean, there's real fruit in those things, right?

Your Attire

Third, if you're the groom, she'll want you to look nice. The easiest way to do this is to wear a tie. The good news is she'll be superimpressed that you dressed up for her. The bad news is, she'll find the tie so fascinating that she'll want to pull, yank, and tighten it until your wife steps in and stops her from choking you.[2]

Dad Lesson

Here's how to tie a tie properly so it's less likely that your daughter will choke you with it when playing wedding. Step 1: Take all of your ties out of the closet. Step 2: Replace them with clip-ons.

Her Attire

Lastly, and most important, your daughter will have a clear picture of what she wants to wear—if you don't get it right, she

---

[2]If you've been sweet to your wife all day, she'll jump in and stop the choking immediately. If you spent the morning reading the *Sports Illustrated* swimsuit issue instead of focusing on other household chores of the day, like taking out the trash or acknowledging that it's her birthday, she'll likely take her time.

may start choosing that boy from daycare over you as groom. That would be bad for you *and* that boy (seriously, don't skip Chapter 12).

In playing wedding with my daughter for the first time, I played the role of the groom (I felt so honored). I had cups ready to "cheers" and Twizzlers ready to eat. My tie hung handsomely from my neck and, to this point, I had only been choked a little. There was only one thing left that she desperately wanted: a wedding dress.

When helping your daughter find a wedding dress, keep in mind that not any dress will suffice. She will have a clear vision of what she wants and will express it to you, in full detail, by saying, "You know, dad, that *one* dress."

"Which one?"

"*That one dress* that I *love.*"

The problem with this statement is that my daughter has a thousand dresses and loves *all* of them. Any one of them could be *that one dress*. So I embarked on a four-hour journey throughout my house, searching high and low (and everywhere else in between) for *that one dress*. I started with the most logical hiding spots, such as her closet and her dresser, pulling out hanger after hanger. It was like a hybrid game, combining hide-and-go-seek with twenty questions, except that there was only one question.

"Is this it?"

"No."

"Is this it?"

"No."

"Is this it?"

"No."

"Is this it?"

"No."

Then, in a move my wife certainly would not approve of, I dug through the dirty laundry in the hamper.[3]

"Is this it?"

"No."

"Is this it?"

"No."

"Is this it?"

"Dad, that's a sock."

"Is that a yes?"

"No."

"Hmm."

Then we hurried back to my daughter's room, where I searched in the toy bin, under her bed, on her bookshelves, in the closet one more time (in case I missed it), and on the ceiling.[4] I still hadn't found it, and my daughter started to look at me as if I had failed her. I missed the game-winning shot. I threw the interception that tied up the game. I broke Cinderella's glass slipper. She had given me one mission—find *that one dress*—and I blew it.

She took me by the hand, like a parent trying to guide a child through a crowded grocery store, and walked me over to *my* dresser. She pulled open one of the drawers. Moments later, it became clear: The wedding dress she wanted to wear was actually one of my white undershirts.

So simple, so sweet. As I put it on her she smiled. Then I smiled. Then I freaked out.

While this seems so adorable (and cheap), don't let it fool you. It is a WEDDING COST INDICATOR!!! She's already thinking in terms of white wedding gowns and, as we all know, white wedding gowns are the most expensive wedding gowns that there

---

[3] Just joking, wife. (Maybe.)

[4] Because one time in college, after a long hunt for my boxers, I found them hanging from a ceiling fan. Never did get to the bottom of that mystery. I'm sure it had something to do with studying too hard.

are. How expensive? I remember when my father-in-law first saw the price tag on my wife's white wedding dress.

"It cost HOW much?" he said as he began to freak out. "I can't believe it cost THAT much. For half that cost, I could hire a rogue CIA gunman and have that groom of yours bumped off. That'd be a hell of a lot cheaper."[5]

EIGHT WAYS TO SAVE FOR YOUR DAUGHTER'S WEDDING

To afford your daughter's wedding, one thing is clear: You are going to need (once you factor in essential amenities, like chair covers and Advil, and twenty-five-years' worth of inflation) about one billion dollars. Don't believe me, see chart below.

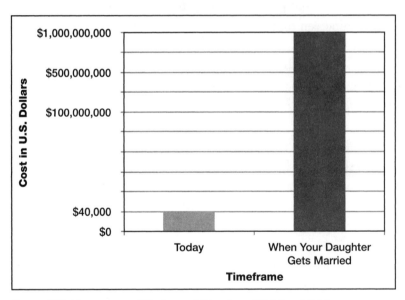

Source: U.S. Department of Budget and Planning—Wedding Division

---

[5]At the time, that statement sounded ludicrous. Now that I'm a dad, the idea seems completely reasonable. Perhaps even preferable.

Saving a billion dollars shouldn't be that hard, right? Thankfully, I have come up with eight different ways you can start raising the funds to pay for your daughter's wedding. I have tried all of them and am well on my way to one billion dollars.[6] Try them out and you'll be on your way soon enough.

1. Start Selling Plasma

No, not TVs. Plasma is the part of your blood that transports water and nutrients to all the cells in the body and is used for transfusions to people who have suffered shock, burns, or visits from The Dad Fairy (see Chapter 12). Each time you donate some, you earn an average of $25. The government allows you to donate up to twice a week, but there is a loophole (article 7, section B of the U.S. law book) that makes an exception for guys with daughters who will eventually have weddings to pay for, and allows them to donate nineteen times a week. At that rate, times fifty-two weeks a year, you should have enough saved by the time she turns seventy, a reasonable age for her to get married.

Also, you are saving lives. This will contribute to the legend of your awesomeness.

2. Mow Lawns

It helped you save up for that pair of Air Jordans back in middle school; now it can help you save up for a wedding. Just make sure you keep your prices under that of the young punk who lives across the street. If you need to, it's completely acceptable to start a rumor that he uses his money to buy heroin. God will forgive you once he hears the sweet melodies of the seventeen-piece orchestra you hired for the church.

---

[6]Only $999,999,800 to go

3. Start a Band

Not only is this fun, but it is also easy. Just get three of your closest friends who have daughters (and excel at Guitar Hero) and off you go. The music doesn't matter nearly as much as your band name. After all, what parish festival wouldn't hire a band named "Shotgun Wedding"?

4. Open a Lemonade Stand

When I was a kid and I wanted to raise a little money, I'd set up a lemonade stand and sell it for 50 cents a glass. Taking into account additional administrative costs (your parents no longer subsidize your expenses and you have to foot the bill for the lemonade packets), marketing costs, a social media presence, and the fact that you can make much better lemonade than you did when you were seven, I think it's reasonable to charge $117 a cup. And that's before the 92 percent Wedding Fund Tax that is applied at the time of sale (pushing the total to $225). But no one carries that much cash, you say? Don't worry. Thanks to smartphone apps and scanners, you can accept all major credit cards.

5. Yell at Little League Umpires

There are plenty of parents in your neighborhood who have kids who play sports. The parents desperately want to yell at the umpires and referees but understand that this is against league policy and any verbal threat toward an umpire will result in immediate ejection from the game. This is where you come in. For a reasonable price, you come to the game dressed as a parent. When given the signal, you rush onto the field and give the umpire hell. You toss your hat, kick dirt on his shoes, wave your hands in the air like a lunatic, etc. This is not only profitable, but fun. Just be careful. I've learned through personal experience that some umpires carry tasers.

6. Sell the Naming Rights to Everything You Own

If sports teams can do this, why can't you? This includes your house, your car, your television, the lamppost in your front yard, your wife's shoe closet and anything else that someone is willing to sponsor. In fact, I made a great deal of money for the six months when I signed a deal with Frito-Lay to change my name to Brian Anthony Nacho Cheese Doritos. It was a glorious six months.

7. Win the Lottery

I know what you're thinking: *But the odds are 175 million to 1 that I will win!* Those are also the same odds that you will be able to afford your daughter's wedding. Coincidence? I highly doubt it. Buy that ticket!

8. Invent Teleporter

Unlike time travel, teleporting is totally possible and it's up to you to invent one. I'm sure someone would pay top dollar to get their hands on one of these puppies—maybe me, as I'll likely need to transport somewhere far, far away when each of my three daughters is ready to get married and comes looking for my credit card.

THE BIG PAYOFF

Like you, I'm still years and years and years and (hopefully) years away from marrying off my daughters. But saving money for their weddings has caused me to spend less time out at the bars and more time at home. I know I could choose to spend the time doing any number of things: eating bacon, eating pork wrapped in bacon, comparing and contrasting the WAR rating of Albert Pujols versus Prince Fielder for a potential fantasy trade while dreaming of eating bacon, etc. But I don't. And I recommend you don't either because this is a prime opportunity to practice for your big moment at your daughter's wedding: The Father/Daughter Dance.

A memorable Father/Daughter Dance takes decades to perfect (another excellent argument in the case to keep her from marrying until she's old enough to become president). There's choosing the right song, practicing the right steps, finding the right bright pink suit that will only modestly embarrass her. Most important, though, you can start practicing with her from the moment she is born. You can hold her up to your cheek and sway back and forth, swaddling her close, letting her know that even if she ever gets married, you will never fully let her go. And when she can walk and start dancing on her own, you'll let her stand on your feet as you waltz around the living room, letting her know that even if she finds someone else to help her through life, she'll still always have you to carry her when she needs it most. And when she's big enough to stand toe-to-toe with you and dance with amazing grace, she'll appreciate how much you love her.

Unfortunately, she will also start to notice that you have no sense of rhythm whatsoever.

Dad Lesson

Never grow new facial hair just before your daughter's wedding. She will not appreciate it. Unless, of course, you are dancing to "Through the Years" by Kenny Rogers. Then grow a totally wicked beard.

Chapter 14

Why Having Daughters Is Really the Best

(DADDY'S GIRL)

As I'm writing this final chapter, I'll have you know that I'm wearing a poofy pink tutu around my waist. Why? My three lovely little ladies—who were shocked (SHOCKED!) to learn that I didn't already own one—made it for me for Christmas so I wouldn't feel "left out" when they wore theirs.

A TUTU? REALLY?

You'd think wearing something so feminine would be embarrassing and humiliating and hard to pull off because, let's face it, a pink tutu doesn't exactly match the collection of jeans, khakis, and ten-year-old concert T-shirts that make up what my wife refers to as "the world's worst wardrobe."[1] You'd think wearing it would cause my wife to leave me because, while tutus look adorable on little girls, they don't quite have the same effect on middle-aged dudes with thinning hairlines and hairy chests. You'd think owning a tutu is something you wouldn't admit publicly, in the back pages of a bestselling book read by millions (thank you!). You'd think a lot of things, but you'd be wrong.

I wear this tutu any time my girls ask me to and I do it proudly—and with a smile on my face.

Allow me to let you in on a little secret: Having a daughter is the best thing that will *ever* happen to you. Period. I don't care if you win the lottery or land the first pick in your upcoming fantasy baseball draft. Having a daughter will open your eyes to a whole new world of love and excitement and experiences that you can't even dream of.

I know I spent much of this book walking you through many of the challenges you'll face while raising a daughter—and you *will*

---

[1] I find it hard to believe she is qualified to make this kind of statement considering 1) I've always dressed like this and she voluntarily agreed to marry me and 2) She still owns several New Kids on the Block T-shirts.

face some challenges along the way. But the big payoff is that you will have a Daddy's Girl. Every father should be so lucky.

As proof that a daughter will actually change your life for the better, here are ten reasons why daughters rule and why you're lucky to have one.

1. EVERYONE AT THE GROCERY STORE PAYS YOU COMPLIMENTS.

Yes, I *know* that you've had people come up to you in the store before to tell you that they've never seen that much handsome on one person until they laid eyes on you. But this is different. Having a daughter is like carrying around a giant magnetic trophy that attracts everyone within eyeshot. They walk right up to you at the deli counter (especially little old ladies) as you're ordering an embarrassing amount of salami,[2] just to let you know how adorable your daughter is. Nearly every conversation goes like this:

"Oh, my, she's simply the most precious thing I've ever seen! How old is she?"

"Eighteen months."

"That's a fun age. I can't believe how beautiful her smile is."

"Thanks."

"She's going to break a lot of hearts when she gets older."

"I sure hope so. Then I won't have to break as many necks."

"You're funny. And handsome. You're wife must be one lucky, lucky lady."

Okay, perhaps I'm paraphrasing here, but you get the point. You will not be able to go out in public without someone doting on your daughter—and this is a good thing. Just by putting a

---

[2]Do you know how much a metric ton is? Me neither. But if I did, it still wouldn't change the fact that I eat a truckload of salami.

bow in her hair and having a daddy/daughter date at the grocery store, you will brighten the days of so many people, including hers. Including *yours*. No one will mention that she's still in her PJs or that you put her shoes on the wrong feet. They will just be glad they bumped into you and had the chance to see that moment.

The world needs more dads who love their daughters so much that they want to show them off to the rest of the world. Be one of those dads and I promise the world will reward you for it.

2. WHEN YOU TELL OTHER GUYS AT THE BAR THAT YOU HAVE A DAUGHTER, THEY BUY YOU A ROUND OUT OF SYMPATHY.

Guys who don't have daughters always assume that having a daughter must be one of the toughest jobs in the world. The more beers they have in them, the more pats you get on the shoulder and the more free drinks you get. It's as if they believe that 90 percent of your life is filled with butterflies and tiaras and "performances" that involve loud tap shoes and even louder renditions of songs that are as new to your daughter as they are to you (because she is making them up on the spot). And you know what? They are 100 percent right. But what they don't know is that you enjoy it—every last second of it.

You'll still love going out to have a few cold ones with your buddies like you always have, but you will also love helping your daughter put on her apron and cooking meat-pickle stew on the stove in her play kitchen. You'll love listening to her stories about her make-believe friends. You'll love giving her zerberts and hugs and carrying her in from the car and putting her to bed after a long day at the park. These moments will create some of the best memories of your life.

And to top it off you get some free beers out of it. Double score.

3. YOU CAN SECRETLY ENJOY LOUSY MUSIC AND CLAIM, "OH, I DON'T LIKE THAT SONG, BUT MY DAUGHTER DOES AND MAKES ME LISTEN TO IT ALL THE TIME."

Daughters are an excellent scapegoat for a number of things: listening to awfully awesome music, going to see cartoon movies in the theater, buying (and reading) *The Sisterhood of the Traveling Pants* (shut up, those books were dynamite). They allow you to do plenty of things you'd normally be too paranoid to try, out of fear you'd get caught and harassed by your friends. Having a daughter gives you a carte blanche excuse to do any girly thing you want with minimal repercussion, so long as you blame it on your daughter.

"Listen, I didn't want to learn the Gangnam Style dance, but my daughter forced me to. She also forced me to record myself doing it, put it on YouTube and give it the thumbs up. Really, I didn't want to, but she forced my hand."

Your daughter won't get upset that you use her as an excuse. In fact, she'll be thrilled that you share in her interests. She will grow up to be a better person because you were involved in her life.

4. ONE DAY, YOU WILL GET TO WALK HER DOWN THE AISLE AT HER WEDDING.

I know, I know, we talked at great length about how much the wedding will cost you. But by the time you are waiting in the back of church or on the beach or wherever your princess decides to get married, that money will have already been spent so you may as well enjoy it.

Walking your daughter down the aisle is one of the most amazing moments that all fathers have to look forward to. It's funny because growing up I never dreamed about my own wedding, but ever since my first daughter was born I've dreamed about hers. I will stare at her in that long, beautiful white gown as she weaves her arm through mine. "Canon in D" begins to play and we make our grand entrance. Lightbulbs flash from every corner of the room, blinding me and causing me to trip and break my arms, immediately postponing the wedding and giving me more time to ~~eliminate the groom~~ prepare for what lies ahead.

I know this is still years down the road, and there will be other special moments that are built just for you and your daughter to share. (I hear some elementary schools hold a Father-Daughter Dance to give you some practice.) Without a daughter, you'd never get those moments. And you'd be missing out—big time.

5. SHE WILL CUDDLE UP WITH YOU WHEN SHE IS SCARED.

Whether it's a loud, exploding sound of thunder or a frightening part in *The Wizard of Oz* (any scene with the Wicked Witch of the West gets my girls) or when some kid comes to the house for Halloween dressed as anything other than a princess, she will run to you, hop on your lap, throw her arms around you, and hold on for dear life. This is because you are her hero.

Disney movies always focus on a prince with some sort of silly sidekick. What Disney should make a movie about is a dad who saves his daughter from things that will ruin her life, like boys who ride motorcycles or a career in journalism. As a dad, you are the person who will protect her when she needs protecting most. This is your job and no matter how hard it seems at times, the truth is, you will love it.

One evening the power went out at our house and all of my daughters were scared. I mean screaming-at-the-top-of-their-lungs scared. My wife and I lit candles and broke out the flashlights, but they still clung to me like I was a giant candy tree. I tried to calm them down by doing shadow puppets on the wall, but it didn't work. I even tried singing the entire soundtrack to *Tangled*, but that only scared them more. Nothing seemed to work. The house only lacked light for nearly thirty minutes, but the way they were acting you'd have thought we'd been sitting in the dark for months. During those long minutes I only had one thought: I hope the power never comes back on.

Your daughter will grow up *way* too fast—trust me. Those moments of her jumping on your lap and clinging tight won't last forever. But your memories of it will. So always hold her close whenever she needs it.

6. SHE WILL ALWAYS LOOK BEAUTIFUL.

From the minute you bring that baby girl home from the hospital she will always look beautiful to you. Even when she has bedhead or is covered in vomit, those eyes and that smile will warm your heart in a way that no one else on this God-given Earth can. You may get upset at times, like when she spills grape juice on your favorite baseball jersey or when she head-butts you in the crotch, but you won't be able to stay mad for more than a few seconds. Why? Every daughter is given a special, "I love you, Daddy" look that she flashes when she knows she's done something wrong. It's an attempt to seek forgiveness. And you know what? It works.

We all need something beautiful in our lives, and when you have a daughter your life will be filled with so much beauty that you'll have extra to share. (Don't worry, it's okay to hog it most of the time.)

7. HAVING A DAUGHTER WILL MAKE YOUR MOM HAPPY, WHICH, IN TURN, MAKES YOU THE BEST SON EVER.

Sure, she's told you before that she loved you more than anything else in the world, but this was a lie. The thing she really loves more than anything in the world is Christmas sweaters that light up. That is, until she has a granddaughter.[3]

There's something magical about watching your mom hold your daughter for the first time. Sure, she'd love a grandson too, but a granddaughter is different. It gives her a chance to buy pretty dresses with headbands to match. It gives her a chance to hand down jewelry that her mother had handed down to her. It gives her a chance to nickname your daughter Curly Q (which drives you crazy) or Angel Baby (which you adore), allowing her to form her own special bond with your daughter. It gives her a chance to see you in action, taking care of your daughter with so much love and affection, gratifying your mom in knowing that she raised you right.

And while she'll never come right out and thank you for giving her a granddaughter, she will drop by your house way too much or pretend to sprain her ankle just so you will bring your daughter over to visit a couple extra times a week. This is her way of showing appreciation.

You're welcome, Mom.

(But seriously, stop with the Curly Q.)

---

[3]A granddaughter is the one person who can appreciate grandma's Christmas sweater that lights up.

8. YOU'LL SEE THE BEST PARTS OF YOUR WIFE IN YOUR DAUGHTER (AND A FEW OF YOUR QUALITIES TOO).

Your wife is an amazing person. She's smart, funny, attractive, caring, and kind. She's also a little crazy. And it's all of these traits that made you fall in love with her.

Having a daughter with her brings the promise of two women who will be smart, funny, attractive, caring, and kind. And a little crazy. Being surrounded by them every day is a blessing, one filled with happiness.

Don't worry, your daughter will pick up some of your finer qualities too, like perfecting the art of the secret handshake and laughing at farts. But she'll be sweeter than you and gentler than you and won't smell as bad as you (usually). A son would smell as bad as you. That's why daughters trump sons, hands down.

9. YOU GET TO PLAY HOOKY WHEN SHE'S SICK.

With a son, you'll ship him to daycare or preschool even if he's running a temperature of 107. With a daughter, you'll call the paramedics if she looks like she's about to produce a mild sneeze. Then your wife will unplug the phones so you can't call the paramedics. Instead, you'll take the day off of work and stay home with her and be whatever she needs. Be it a soup-maker or book reader or a pillow to lie on, you'll transform into a superhero who will heal your daughter one cup of juice at a time.

One challenging weekend, all of my daughters caught a stomach bug on the same day. My wife wanted to help, but she had the bug too. So I swooped into action, surrounding them with pots and pans so that no matter which way they puked, they'd almost certainly still get the carpet. I rushed each one of them to the bathroom so many times that I qualified for one of those marathon bumper stickers that reads 26.2. I also lost fourteen pounds. When their fevers finally broke, I was there to wipe the sweat from their foreheads—just like any good dad would.

Taking care of a sick daughter and knowing you are there for her when she needs you most is 1,000 times more gratifying than any job could ever deliver.

10. NO MATTER HOW BAD YOUR DAY IS GOING, HER HUGS AND KISSES WILL MAKE IT ALL BETTER.

You could be experiencing the worst day. Perhaps your close ally at work is leaving for a better job and, instead of replacing him, your company has just decided to dump all his work on you. To make matters worse, your car got sideswiped in the parking lot and the sideswiper[4] didn't even have the courtesy to leave a note. Then on the ride home, your wife tells you that she broke your Xbox. And your favorite band broke up. And your mother-in-law is moving in with you.

This nightmare would cause most men to off themselves. But not you, now that you have a daughter.

When I'm having an awful day I count down the minutes until I see my girls. The second they see me they come running up as fast as they can and jump into my arms. Their hugs and their kisses erase everything—work, car damage, the indigestion from eating forty Chicken McNuggets at lunch. I ask them how their days were and they tell me "Better now that you're here." It makes me melt. And when your daughter cures your ails with her hugs and her kisses, it'll melt you too.

---

[4]Swiper, no swiping!

Now that you are in the club and know all the tricks of the trade, you will be able to enjoy these special times with your daughter without as much stress as you probably had before reading this book. I hope you've learned a valuable lesson.[5] I also hope you spread the gospel to other dads out there who are staring in the face of the life-altering experience that is known as having a daughter. You want them to know that when the doctor says, "Oh boy, you're having a girl," their life isn't over. It's only just beginning. And it's going to be amazing.

Of course, this chapter becomes null and void the minute they hit their teenage years. Then, good luck and Godspeed.

---

[5]The Cincinnati Bengals will win next year's Super Bowl. Call Vegas now.

Chapter 15

Surviving Fatherhood Emergencies

(DO NOT OPEN THIS CHAPTER
UNLESS IT'S AN EMERGENCY)

Oh shit, you opened this chapter? I was really hoping that you wouldn't have to. If you had to open it, then I feel for you, I really do. Because no matter how prepared you are, your daughter will still throw curveballs at you from time to time. Luckily, I can anticipate what kind of curveball she will throw at you (I've been scouting the pitches thrown by daughters for a number years), and I can give you the methods to get you out of these pickles.

This chapter covers three all-too-common daughter emergency scenarios. I've experienced every one of them and am living proof that they won't kill you (though, if you're not prepared, they will cause a reasonable amount of psychological damage . . . and impotence). Don't worry, though, I will walk you through these scenarios and offer specific instructions on how to handle them and prevent these emergencies from getting out of control.

EMERGENCY #1: UNEXPECTED GUESTS

You are having a nice, quiet afternoon with your daughter when she suggests you have a tea party. Not only does *she* want to dress up, but she wants *you* to dress up as well, so she covers you from head to toe in bows, tiaras, stickers, and glitter. You sit down and begin to drink your tea out of the Disney Cinderella cup your daughter has filled specifically for you. All is right in her world, so all is right in your world.

Then comes a knock at your door. You excuse yourself from the party for a moment to answer it. You open the door to find several of your close friends standing there (you had completely forgotten that they were picking you up to watch the big game at a local pub with them). The giant grins and snickers on their faces cause you to have a revelation: *OH, GOD, I CURRENTLY LOOK LIKE A PRINCESS!*

What do you do?

Solution:

First of all, don't panic. Your friends are good at sensing fear. And the more they sense, the worse this situation will get. There is nearly nothing you can do to save face in front of your friends and if you act embarrassed, you will break your little girl's heart (which is completely unacceptable). So instead of standing there and taking a ribbing from your friends, I recommend doing this:

"Oh, thank goodness, you guys are finally here."

(You turn and look at your daughter.) "Hey, sweetie, the *rest* of the tea party guests are here. I'll go start grabbing the bows and glitter. Did you make enough for everyone?"

By the time you turn back around, your porch will be empty. Problem solved, right? WRONG!

At least one of the guys snapped a picture of you on his smartphone and will upload it to Facebook within the next five minutes. You need to get ahead of the "scandal" by taking a quick picture of you and your daughter enjoying your tea together and posting it first. Make sure you use the caption, "My daughter makes the best pretend tea in the world! I'm so happy to share it with her!"

Before any of your buddies can leave snarky comments, each one of their wives will not only "like" the photo but will leave comments like, "How adorable!" and "You're the best dad in the world!" and "Jeff does the same thing, only our daughter also makes him wear earings!"

And now the focus is on Jeff.

You're welcome.

EMERGENCY #2: DRAFT SCHEDULE CONFLICT

Your daughter has a ballet recital at the same time as your annual fantasy football draft. You've done your best to get the draft moved, but the other members of your league have no interest in doing you any favors (partly because you've won three of the past five years and, in an effort to rub it in a little, you may or may not have started a petition to rename the league trophy after yourself), so they refuse. You absolutely *cannot* miss your daughter's ballet recital (even if her dance routine lasts a grand total of four minutes somewhere in the middle of the godforsaken three-hour event). If you tried to skip, your daughter (and your wife) would never forgive you.

Solution:

Send your dad to the fantasy draft in your place and equip him with an intricate matrix of draft scenarios and picks that you want him to take depending on which scenario unfolds. Your dad will be so happy that *he* doesn't have to go to the recital that he may even offer to cover half of your league fees. SCORE!

NOTE: Admittedly, this play isn't 100 percent guaranteed to work. There is a slight chance that your dad will use every pick on Terry Bradshaw (who was *his* favorite player as a kid). But if you want to keep the ladies in your life happy, it's a risk you'll have to take.

EMERGENCY #3: YOUR WIFE WANTS ANOTHER BABY

Your wife is already talking about having *another* baby. This can happen when your daughter is a few years old. It can happen when she's still a newborn. Hell, I once heard a wife mention having another baby in front of her husband while she was still pregnant (and he was still dealing with the news that they were having a daughter!). This is worrisome because, if you already have a daughter, you have a 98 percent chance that your next child will also be a daughter.[1] So what do you do?

---

[1] This stat is furnished by the American Medical Association's Department of Pregnancy, Births, and Louis Vuitton Handbags. It is also sponsored by Macy's.

Solution:

Give in. Daughters are awesome.

FINAL QUIZ

You've made it! The end of the book is here and I promise that you are now smarter and more equipped to handle raising a daughter than ever before. And, somehow, you are even more handsome!

To test your new wealth of knowledge, I'm giving you one final ten-question quiz that will not only challenge you on your parenting skills (which I'm sure you've mastered because, like me, you have a daughter—and this, my friend, makes you 100 percent awesome) but will also build your confidence when you achieve a perfect score.[1]

Plus, as you know from the earlier quiz, the answers are all still D.

---

[1]This quiz is graded on the curve. The minimum you can score is 100 percent. Feel free to rip these pages out, write a giant "100%" on it, and hang it on your fridge. You've earned it (just by having a daughter).

You're in a stall in the men's bathroom helping your daughter go potty when she looks up at you and loudly says, "Dad, why does the person in the potty next to ours smell like farts?" You:

A. Calmly explain to her that this is a bathroom and that everything in it smells like farts.
B. Tell her not to worry about anything other than not peeing on your shoes.
C. In an effort to diffuse the situation, take the rap by saying, "Sorry, hon, that was me. I farted. I smell like farts."
D. Laugh uncontrollably. After all, it's pretty funny.

You are sitting on the couch with your daughter when, out of nowhere, she mentions that her belly hurts and suddenly throws up in your lap. You:

A. Immediately call 911 and tell the operator that you need medical attention stat because your daughter is exploding all over you.
B. Look her right in the eye and say, "Don't worry, sweetie. You're full of so much awesome your little body can't contain it and it's trying to escape."
C. Commiserate with her by throwing up in your wife's lap.
D. Call your mom and ask her to take care of the both of you. She's an expert at cleaning up puke and caring for a pukey child. She'll also bring you amazing chicken soup, because that's what moms do.

You've been asked by your daughter to be the groom in her pretend wedding. You accept by saying:

A. "Of course! I would love to marry you. But you better clear it with your mom first, as I don't want her to get jealous."

B. "Am I allowed to stay in my PJs or do I need to get dressed up?"

C. "Can I continue to eat my meatball hoagie?"

D. "Sure, under one condition: This is the last time you *ever* get married."

Your daughter, who apparently got up in the middle of the night and peeked in your room, asks you why you and your wife were naked in bed the other night. Your response is:

A. "Mom forgot to do the laundry . . . AGAIN!"

B. "You were just having a dream, sweetheart. If you ever have that dream again, it's best to turn around, go back to bed, and never, ever mention it to anyone."

C. "The air conditioning broke in our room only, so we took off our clothes in an attempt to cool off."

D. "Your mom wanted to see which one of us was hairier. It was definitely me—hands down."

You're on a Daddy-Daughter date at her favorite restaurant when she has to go potty. You rush her to the public restroom and break one of the rules on your wife's "Under No Circumstances List." Do you tell your wife?

A. Yes, because you are in a committed relationship that is based on honesty.
B. Yes, but you stay as general as you can without going into any detail. You also take your daughter upstairs and immediately give her a bath.
C. Yes, but only because you know there's absolutely no way your daughter can keep the secret.
D. Not if you value your life.

Your friends call and ask you to join them at a strip club for your buddy Mark's bachelor party. You:

A. Tell them you have no interest in strip clubs and politely decline.
B. Tell them you have no interest in strip clubs and politely decline.
C. Tell them you have no interest in strip clubs and politely decline.
D. Doesn't matter. You can't answer the phone because you're too busy cleaning up a pool of daughter diddle on the bathroom floor where, to be just like you, she tried to pee standing up.

In front of all your friends, your daughter asks you when she will grow a penis. Your gut reaction is to:

A. Fake a heart attack and hope that the ambulance comes quickly enough before she tries to ask you something more embarrassing, like, "Will it come with balls?"

B. Fake a stroke and hope that she'll pity you enough to drop the inquisition.

C. Pretend like you didn't hear the question.

D. Turn to your friends and say, "I need a little help here. When did *your* daughters grow their penises?

You've tried everything within your power to get your daughter to pee on the potty but nothing works. Do you:

A. Give up and hope they make diapers in a size 17.

B. Hire a professional to teach her how to do it.

C. Pray for a miracle.

D. Paint the potty to look like a giant diaper, hoping to confuse her.

You notice a particular boy has been playing house with your daughter an awful lot and your daughter has taken quite a liking to him. One day, he "unexpectedly" disappears. Your daughter asks you what happened to him and you tell her:

A. "I have no idea, sweetie. Perhaps he moved away. Far, far away."
B. "Boys are like that, sweetie. They just come and go, which is why you can never trust any boys other than me. I will never, ever leave you. I pinky promise."
C. "What boy? I don't ever remember there being a boy around here. Perhaps you were imagining him?"
D. "The less you know, the better."

QUESTION 10

Your daughter tells you that you're her favorite daddy in the whole wide world. You:

A. Hug her with all your might.
B. Kiss her.
C. Tell her that you love her more than you love anything else in the world, including bacon.[2]
D. All of the above.

---

[2]This is the highest compliment you can pay anyone.

Appendix

At This Age: What Girls Are Learning

0-6 MONTHS

Language
- Knows how to scream. Loudly.
- Starts to communicate with smiles. This either means she is happy or is about to pass gas.

Cognitive/Intellectual
- Learns to suck on anything she thinks can dispense food, like boobs, bottles, pacifiers and, if you get it too close to her, your nose.
- Doesn't understand that daytime is for playing and nighttime is for sleeping.
- Loves to be held close, unlike your wife who prefers you stay at least ten feet away from her postpartum party.

Physical/Motor
- Starts to hold head up instead of dangling it from her neck like an Olympic medal.
- Begins to roll over, from back to belly and belly to back. Unfortunately she will not do this on command, like a dog, so don't expect her to impress your friends.
- Practices sitting up.
- Practices falling over from sitting up.
- Gains the ability to accidentally poke you in the eye. (Watch out for this one, it hurts!)

Self-Care
- HA!

6-12 MONTHS

Language
- Starts to "coo" a lot. This is parent speak for "keeps me up at night."
- Might say her first word, though it's not really a word, but a belch that happens to sound like "dad."

Cognitive/Intellectual
- Recognizes that you exist and are, in fact, in the room with her.
- Cries less when in mom's arms because she doesn't want your wife to feel bad that, even at this young age, your daughter realizes that you are the most awesome person in the world.

Physical/Motor
- Learns how to crawl.
- Learns how to crawl really, really fast.
- Learns how to knock things over, including your prized Pete Rose bobblehead. (Dammit.)
- Takes her first step, which means you will never be able to sit down again.

Self-Care
- Double HA!

12–18 MONTHS

Language

- Responds to own name. Also responds to terms of endearment, such as "princess," "sweetheart," and "stinky."
- Responds to one-step commands (e.g., "Come here." "Stay there." "Don't eat that booger.")
- Doesn't respond to one-word commands (e.g., "Stop," "No," or "Nooooooooooo!")
- Communicates needs (such as needing her diaper changed or needing you to clean up the diaper she already tried to change and smeared up and down her crib) by pointing and making sounds.
- Knows the meaning of "mama," "dada," "Dora," and "on-base percentage."
- Repeats words and imitates sounds, especially naughty words you accidentally used around her. In fact, she's kind of like a parrot who likes to stick out her tongue and go "pbbbbt"...and then yell "boobs."
- Points to a part of the body, like your nose hair.
- Jabbers, hums, and "sings" at least two '80s TV theme show songs.
- Identifies the difference between two images in books, like a dog and a cat, a car and a train, a Vera Wang gown and an off-the-rack dress.

Cognitive/Intellectual

- Understands that a hidden object still exists until you say abracadabra.
- Repeats actions to learn that cause (raised hand) leads to effect (high five).
- Explores every toy in your house via touch and taste.

- Sorts simple objects by shape and size (e.g., tiny hiney, teeny tiny hiney, badonkadonk).
- Dumps things out, especially liquids that stain your carpet.
- Takes things out of a container (your wallet) and puts them back in (though mysteriously your credit cards remain missing).

Physical/Motor

- Stands alone.
- Puts an object in a container.
- Puts object in mouth.
- Puts object up nose.
- Lowers herself from standing to sitting (also known as "practicing the wave").
- Scribbles (on your work shirts).
- Walks alone (as punishment for scribbling on your work shirts).
- Opens drawers and cabinets, mainly ones that you spent hours installing safety latches on.
- Bends over and picks something up (this is the last time she will ever pick anything up in your house again).
- Throws a ball (splitfinger).
- Claps (at your favorite sports team).
- Points with index finger (at your favorite sports team's terrible bullpen).
- Climbs one–two foot objects without even considering that you are afraid of heights.

Self-Care

- Washes hands (good).
- Drinks from a cup with a lid (good).
- Takes off an article of clothing (very, very bad).

18–24 MONTHS

Language
- Understands the meaning of "don't" but chooses to ignore it.
- Speaks in gibberish that has the cadence and rhythm of your twenty-first birthday celebration.
- Knows names for familiar people, including Stephen, your HDTV.
- Uses fifty words to describe her dream wedding.
- Makes two-word sentences ("I eat," "I poop").
- Listens to short books (*Moneyball*) and nursery rhymes (*Moneyball*, but done in a singsong voice).
- Points to six parts of the body when asked, which may earn her a college scholarship considering she only has two hands.

Cognitive/Intellectual
- Understands categories (e.g., "toys," "books," "foods," "RBIs").
- Pretends (e.g., the piece of Play Doh is a snake, the piece of Play Doh is a worm, the piece of Play Doh is a snake pretending to be a worm).
- Points to specific pictures (of you) in (photo album) books when asked (who is her favorite parent).
- Focuses on an activity for five minutes (this is not true).
- Tries different ways to ignore you.
- Chooses between two things (drafting a quarterback and drafting a running back).

Physical/Motor
- Runs.
- Walks up steps.
- Stacks six blocks.
- Kicks a ball forward (and it's not an accident!).

Social

- Lets you know her favorite word to say is "no."
- Handles simple responsibilities like losing the remote.
- Feels concerned when you are crying—understands why when she looks at the score of the game.
- Is interested in other children (dear God, don't let it be boys).
- Tries to comfort someone (you) who is very upset (discovered your wife's credit card bill).
- Feeds a doll Play Doh.

Self-Care

- Uses a spoon and fork to throw food on the floor (thank goodness—she used to do it barbarically with her hands).
- Puts on an article of clothing (that's more like it!).
- Puts arms and legs through correct holes when being dressed, a feat not even her father has mastered.

24–36 MONTHS

Language

- Speaks in two- to four-word sentences, such as "stop singing, Dad" and "stop singing Dad, seriously."
- Has short conversations with her imaginary friend, Jennifer.

Cognitive/Intellectual

- Listens to books with simple stories, so long as you are willing to read the same ones over and over and over and over again.
- Identifies one color (pink).
- Understands the concepts "one" and "two" and "threepeat."

Physical/Motor

- Draws pictures of unicorns (or a tugboat, it's really hard to tell).
- Kicks a ball forward (okay, this time it was an accident).
- Throws a ball (like a girl, though).
- Stands on one foot to do *Karate Kid* Crane Kick.
- Stands on tiptoes to knock something over.
- Goes up and down stairs using alternate ways of falling.
- Climbs low ladders (wait, why are you leaving low ladders out?).
- Pedals a tricycle and is (finally) able to drive herself to ballet.

Social

- Plays next to other children so long as they are also wearing princess dresses.
- Starts using the term BFF.
- Categorizes people as superheros and fairies.
- Participates in interactive games like "Duck, Duck, Goose!" and "Pull My Finger."
- Identifies a friend as someone whom her dad will kill if that "friend" is also a "boy."

Self-Care

- Starts to use the potty (Woohoo!).
- Brushes her own hair . . . and yours, which is way more painful than you expect.
- Puts on pants—she no longer needs you. Your job here is done.

Acknowledgments

This book wouldn't have been possible without the help of an incredibly supportive and patient team of people. First and foremost, I'd like to thank my wife, Brittany, who supports me no matter how crazy I sound or how big I dream. She puts up with a lot—thankfully, I reward her with being so handsome. I'd also like to thank my mom, who is one of the most creative people I know and has been supportive of my writing ever since she helped me write my first short story when I was in sixth grade. I hope I am as wonderful to my daughters as you are to me. I'd like to thank my sister, Jennie; my grandparents, Frank and Marlene and Clem and Jane; and my in-laws, Kevin and Denise; who have always believed in me even when I didn't believe in myself. That meant the world to me.

Other thank yous go out to my agent, Tina Wexler, who works harder than anyone I know and is 1,000 times cooler than I am; Laura Daly, who gave me great feedback and really helped make this book funnier; and Brendan O'Neill, for being an all-around amazing editor. Seriously, he's an idea machine. He's also patient, smart, funny, and good-looking (probably).

I'd also like to extend my gratitude to Chuck and Zac. If it weren't for our brilliant brainstorming over delicious lunches, I'd probably be a lot thinner. I'd also probably give up on too many good ideas. I appreciate the fact that you never let me. And to all my loving family, friends, teachers, TheLifeOfDad.com fans and anyone else who has played even a minor role in my life, thank you from the bottom of my heart.

It's also important that I thank my dad. He taught me everything I know about humor, love, and being awesome. He was the world's greatest father and role model, and I try to emulate him every day of my life. I really, really wish he could have hung around on this beautiful Earth long enough to see me publish this book. He would have been so proud. I can only hope that there's a bookstore in heaven and that he's holding a copy right now, bragging to his angel friends.

And finally, I want to give the biggest thank you to my daughters, Ella, Anna, and Mia. You mean everything to me and I'm so thankful you are in my life. I love you so much. When you grow up I will support you and will work hard every day to help you chase your dreams too—even if your dream is to write a book about your crazy dad.

Index

manliness challenges. *See* Eight
Challenges of Sheer Manliness
other guy with daughter, 53–55
quiz question, 106
reacting to birth of your girl,
48–50
strip club request by, 199
sympathy rounds from, 180
watching how you handle having
daughter, 55

Games
board, 64–67
manly. *See* Eight Challenges of
Sheer Manliness
Genitals, questions/answers, 117,
200
Girls. *See also* Birth of daughter;
specific topics
father's perspective on having,
13–15
mistaken as boys, 35–36
reasons they're the best. *See*
Daughters, why they're the best
Grass-Cutting Faceoff challenge,
53
Grief stages, pink world and, 33–35
about: overview of, 33
acceptance, 35
anger, 34
bargaining, 34
denial and isolation, 34
depression, 34
Grill Off! challenge, 51–52, 106
Guests, unexpected, 190–91

Halftime quiz, 101–7
Halloween, Disney and, 61–63
Homecoming, after birth of daughter, 26–27

Hugging/kissing your daughter,
115, 122, 131, 180, 186–87, 201

Illness. *See* Sickness and injury
In-laws, bonding with father-in-
law, 24–25

The Karate Kid–style lessons (for
dressing girls), 39–41
about: overview of, 39–40
picking out clothes and, 41
vacuuming carpet and, 40
washing dishes and, 41
washing laundry and, 40
Kidney transplant scenario, 125

Language development
0–6 months, 204
6–12 months, 205
12–18 months, 206
18–24 months, 208
24–36 months, 210
Laundry, *Karate Kid*–style lesson, 40
Lawns, mowing, 172
Lemonade stand, opening, 173
Lessons. *See* Dad Lessons
Letter, to daughter's crushes,
158–62
Life-threatening disease, dealing
with, 125
Lottery, winning, 174

Manliness challenges. *See* Eight
Challenges of Sheer Manliness
Map, Dora and, 72, 78
Mom (of your daughter). *See* Wife
Mom (yours), daughter making
happy, 184

ABOUT THE AUTHOR

BRIAN A. KLEMS is a writer, editor, husband, perennial fantasy sports underachiever, and father of three girls. He's a proud graduate of the E.W. Scripps journalism school at Ohio University. He's also the online editor of *Writer's Digest* magazine.

Brian writes an award-winning parenting blog, TheLifeOfDad .com, for the *Cincinnati Enquirer*, which was named one of the Best Parent Blogs in Ohio by Moms Trusted. His writing has appeared in dozens of print and online periodicals, including *Southern MOMentum, Family Friendly Cincinnati, OC Family*, and more.

His *Writer's Dig* blog (*writersdigest.com/online-editor*)—which covers writing and publishing—is one of the fastest growing blogs in the writing community, while his Questions & Quandaries column has appeared in *Writer's Digest* for nearly a decade.

When he's not writing, Brian loves reading, playing softball, losing to his wife at Words with Friends, and laughing. You can find him on Twitter @BrianKlems, on his parenting blog (*www .TheLifeOfDad.com*), or at Great American Ballpark with his daughters, cheering on his Cincinnati Reds.